Folens History Book 4

Technology, War and Identities

A World Study After 1900

Aaron Wilkes

Author's acknowledgements

The author wishes to acknowledge Peter Burton and Nina Randall of Folens Publishers for their advice during the preparation of this book. He is particularly indebted to his wife, Emma, and daughter, Hannah, for the support they have given. He also wishes to recognise the efforts of Mr Day and Mr Kirby, two of the author's own history teachers, whose enthusiasm for their subject inspired him more than they know. The author dedicates this book to his late friend, Alex Dunkley (1972–2003), a man who was endlessly fascinated by the intrigue of modern world history.

United Kingdom: Folens Publishers, Apex Business Centre, Boscombe Road, Dunstable, LU5 4RL.

Email: folens@folens.com

Ireland: Folens Publishers, Greenhills Road, Tallaght, Dublin 24.

Email: info@folens.ie

Poland: JUKA, ul. Renesansowa 38, Warsaw 01-905.

Editor: Nina Randall

Series design, page layout and illustrations: Neil Sutton, Pumpkin House Cambridge

Picture researcher: Sue Sharp

Cover design: 2idesign Ltd., Cambridge

First published 2004 by Folens Limited.

British Library Cataloguing in Publication Data. A catalogue record for this publication is available from the British Library.

ISBN 1 84303 411 5

Acknowledgements

Aaron Wilkes: 20; akg-images, London: 76, 81, 84, 97, 100/101, 122; Art Archive: 106; Art Archive/Bibiotheque des Arts Decoratifs Paris/Marc Charmet: 23; Associated Press: 110, 127, 132/133; Bridgeman Art Library: 121; British Pathe Plc/ITN Archive: 44; Centre for the Study of Cartoons and Caricature, University of Kent/ Vicky/Evening Standard/Solo: 107; Collection of Tonie & Valmai Holt: 83; Corbis: 18; Corbis/Bettmann: 98, 105, 109, 112, 113, 124; Corbis/David Pollack: 108; Corbis/Hulton Deutsch Collection: 16, 90; Corbis/NASA: 117; Dudley Archives & Local History Service (A620 Hingley of Netherton): 10; Getty Images London/Stereoscopic Company: 4 (bottom); Getty Images London/Time Inc: 128; Hulton Archive/Getty Images London: 24, 56, 63; Imperial War Museum: 26 (all), 30, 31, 34, 36, 37, 49, 53, 71, 87, 93, 96, 102; Janet Booth: 45; Liverpool Record Office, Liverpool Libraries & Information Services (352 HOU 82/16): 4 (top); London Metropolitan Archives (IMA): 9; Mary Evans Picture Library: 12, 52 (both), 55, 65, 66, 69, 70, 73, 74, 116, 123; Mirror Syndication: 48; NASA: 118; NI Syndication: 130; People's History Museum: 115; Peter Newark's Military Pictures: 89, 95; Popperfoto: 64, 75, 134; Robert Hunt Library: 41; Topham Picturepoint: 5, 79; Wiener library, Institute of Contemporary History: 99.

'All Quiet On The Western Front' (video) 1930: 29; 'A Victorian Son: An Autobiography 1897–1922' by Stuart Cloete, J Day Co. 1973: 35; 'Britain 1906–1918' by Richard Radway, Hodder & Stoughton, 2002: 5; 'Children at War' by the BBC, 1989: 105; 'Emperor's Guest, 1942-45' by John Fletcher-Cooke, Hutchinson , 1971: 106; 'GCSE Modern World History' by Ben Walsh, John Murray, 1996: 79; 'Hitler's Germany' by Josh Brooman, Longman, 1991: 77; 'Investigating History' by Neil De Marco, Hodder & Stoughton, 2003: 100; 'Keep Smiling Through: Women in the Second World War' by Caroline Lang, Cambridge University Press, 1989: 91; 'Poverty: A Study of Town Life' by S Rowntree, 1901: 8; 'SHP Peace and War' by Shephard, Reid and Shephard, John Murray, 1993: 88, 91, 92, 96 (X2), 105; 'The Great War: First World War, 1914–18' by Josh Brooman, Longman, 1985: 40; 'The Suffragette Movement: An Intimate Account of Persons and Ideas' by Sylvia Pankhurst, Virago Press, 1977: 55; 'The Twentieth Century' by JD Clare, Nelson Thornes, 1993: 64; 'Twentieth Century World (Foundation)' by Fiona Reynoldson, Heinemann, 1995: 97; 'Weimar and Nazi Germany' by Fiona Reynoldson, Heinemann, 1996: 78; 'Weimar Germany' by Josh Brooman, Longman, 1985: 65; 'With a Machine Gun to Cambrai' by George Coppard, HMSO, 1969: 27; 'www.badastronomy.com': 119; 'www.redzero.demon.co.uk': 118 (X2).

Contents

Introduction

Into the twentieth century   4

1   A changing world   8

Why do we have school dinners?   8

Titanic tour   10

History Mystery: why did *Titanic* sink?   14

What can the *Titanic* tell us?   16

2   The Great War   20

Why did the Great War start?   20

Joining up   26

3   What was it like to fight?   28

Trench warfare   28

Trench life   32

The world's deadliest weapons, 1914   36

Were the 'lions' *really* 'led by donkeys'?   40

Shot at Dawn: the story of Private
Harry Farr   44

How did 'Poppy Day' start?   48

Have you been learning?   50

4   Between the wars   52

How did women win the vote?   52

History Mystery: Emily Davison
– suicide or protest?   54

How did countries try to avoid any
more wars?   56

Different ways to run a country   58

Two types of dictatorship   60

5   The Nazis   64

Adolf Hitler – choirboy, artist, tramp,
soldier, politician   64

Why were the Nazis so popular?   68

Life in Nazi Germany   72

The Olympic Games, 1936   78

Have you been learning?   80

6   World War Two   82

Why was there another world war?   82

Who were the 'Few'?   86

'Mr and Mrs Jones would like a nice
little boy'   90

Sir Arthur Harris: war hero or war
criminal?   94

What was Auschwitz like?   98

The end of World War Two: why were
nuclear bombs used?   104

7   Modern times   108

United Nations?   108

Why don't we pay to see a doctor?   114

History Mystery: man on the moon …
or was he?   116

Whatever happened to the British
Empire?   120

The Rosa Parks story   126

What Is terrorism?   130

8   Looking forward, looking back   136

Into the twenty-first century   136

Have you been learning?   140

Glossary   142

Index   144

Into the twentieth century

▶ What was Britain's status in world affairs in 1900?
▶ What was Britain itself like?

In 1900, the British people had every reason to be proud. For a start, most Brits were better fed, clothed, healthier and more educated than many of the people of other nations of the world. Cities were full of shops that contained a wide range of goods, either made in British factories or brought in from parts of their Empire. In 1900, Britain controlled over a quarter of the world (about 400 million people) and was the largest empire the world had ever seen.

▼ **Source A** A popular British song from 1900

> *'We don't want to fight,*
> *but by jingo if we do,*
> *we've got the ships,*
> *we've got the men,*
> *we've got the money too.'*

▼ **Source B** These two photographs highlight the contrast between rich and poor in 1900. They were taken only a few days and a few miles apart, yet the poor slum area is vastly different from the rich Park Lane region of London. How can you tell which one is poor and which one is rich?

Yet Britain had its fair share of problems. The United States was now making more goods than Britain and Germany was quickly catching up. Could Britain hold on to its position as the country that did more trade (and made more money) than any other? Despite having more battleships than any other two nations added together, there were some serious rivals for position of 'top dog'. France had a big army and Germany's was one of the largest and best trained that Europe had ever seen. These countries were just as proud of themselves as the British were. Could this rivalry lead to war?

So what was Britain like at the beginning of the twentieth century?

Queen Victoria died on the evening of Monday 22 January 1901. She had been Queen for 63 years. Her son, Edward, became Edward VII. Through her marriage to Albert, and the marriages of her children, Britain's Royal Family became connected to the rulers of countries such as Russia, Germany, Spain, Norway and Sweden.

In 1900, one writer claimed that the lives led by the rich and the poor were so different that Britain was like two nations – a poor nation and a rich one. About 3% were very rich (upper class), 25% were relatively wealthy (middle-class bankers, doctors, accountants, managers and so on) and the rest were very poor (working class).

▼ **Source C** Adapted from a report by Jack London, an American writer who visited the East End of London in 1900.

'The streets were filled with a new and different type of people, short and of a beer-soaked appearance. At a market, tottery old men were searching the garbage thrown in the mud for rotten potatoes, beans and vegetables, while children clustered like flies around a rotten mass of fruit, twisting their arms into the mouldy mess and bringing out decaying scraps, which they devoured on the spot.'

By 1900, many women were demanding the freedom to do something useful with their lives. More and more didn't want to fit into the role of the dutiful wife and mother. Some found jobs in nursing, typing or teaching for example ... and paid taxes to a Government they couldn't even vote for! Some women were demanding another type of freedom too. They wanted to wear clothing that didn't restrict their movements so much. By 1900, women's clothing was getting looser, but the woman's corset was still very popular (see **Source E**). This item of underwear pulled in the waist and pushed up the rest! Most women hated it ... but wore it to please their man. Some corsets pulled a woman's waist in to 15 inches – measure it yourself!

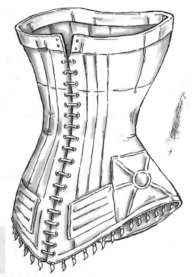

▶ **Source E** A woman's corset

▼ **Source D** Shopping habits were beginning to change in the early 1900s. Instead of shopkeepers selling just a few similar items, they would sell a wide range of different items in separate departments – the department store was born. This photograph of 'The Stores' in Taunton, Somerset, was taken in 1904. You can see the shopkeeper is trying to attract shoppers by offering many different products. By 1910, he would be able to offer Coca-Cola (arrived from the US in 1900), Marmite (1902), Heinz Baked Beans (1904), Gillette razors (1904), Kellogg's Corn Flakes (1906), Hoover vacuum cleaners (1907) and Persil washing powder (1909).

FACT: ▶ Read all about it!

▶ The early 1900s saw the birth of some of Britain's now familiar newspapers.

In 1896, the *Daily Mail* had begun the idea of short easy-to-read articles, accompanied by gossip, sports stories, horse racing tips, fashion news and advertisements. It was followed by the *Daily Express* (1900), the *Daily Mirror* (1903) and *The Sun* (1911).

▼ **Source F** Cadbury's Dairy Milk was launched in 1905. It was going to be called Cadbury's Dairy Maid but the name was changed six weeks before it went on sale.

In 1884, Karl Benz, a German, made the first successful petrol-driven vehicle. It had three wheels and could reach speeds of up to ten miles per hour. In 1887, Gottlieb Daimler, another German, made the first four-wheeled petrol-driven car.

By 1900, car-making had become a big moneymaking industry but cars were still too expensive for most people. Then, in 1909, an American called Henry Ford began making what was to become one of the best-selling cars ever – the Model T Ford. Based in Detroit, USA, the Henry Ford Motor Company had made over one million by 1915. Ford used state-of-the-art techniques in his factory to **mass-produce** them on an **assembly line**. The cars would pass in front of the workers on a conveyor belt and each person would have an individual job to do. The cars were made quickly ... and cheaply. In fact, in 1909, a Model T cost $950 to buy, but by 1927, Ford was making them so efficiently that the price dropped to $290.

▼ **Source G** Ford's Model T car, nicknamed 'Tin Lizzie'. Ford's first British factory opened in Manchester in 1911.

FACT: ▶ Not so fast

▶ Along with the motor car came the motor car driving offence. In 1896, Walter Arnold from Kent became the first British driver to be fined for speeding. He was caught doing eight miles per hour in a two miles per hour zone.

On 17 December 1903, in North Carolina, USA, Orville Wright made the first man-carrying powered flight. It lasted 12 seconds and he flew a distance of 37 metres. His brother, Wilbur, had helped to build the aeroplane. By 1905, the brothers had made nearly 300 flights, some lasting nearly 20 minutes. Flying became the latest craze and in 1909, a Frenchman, Louis Bleriot, flew over the English Channel. By 1910, some countries were looking into the possibility of attaching bombs to planes so they could be dropped on an enemy!

▼ **Source H** The first modern Olympic Games were held in Athens, Greece, in 1896. The second Games were held in Paris four years later. The 1900 Olympics were the first to allow women to compete. Perhaps times were changing! This is a copy of the poster for the 1900 Games.

Sport remained as popular after 1900 as it had been in the previous century. Football, cricket, rugby, tennis and golf continued to attract thousands of spectators and participants. Cycling was as popular a sport as any – in 1900, there were more than 2,000 cycling clubs in Britain!

FACT: ▶ Good old Teddy

▶ The first teddy bears were made in the United States in 1903. They were named after US President Teddy Roosevelt who refused to shoot a bear whilst out on a hunting trip.

(!) WISE UP WORDS

mass-production   assembly line

FACT: ▶ Curie's cure

▶ In 1898, Polish scientist Marie Curie discovered the element radium. It was soon found that radium destroyed diseased cells and so was used in cancer therapy. What wasn't known was that, without protection, radium could make the air radioactive, cause radiation sickness and permanently damage the body. Curie died after working for 25 years without protection – yet her work has helped to save and prolong the lives of millions of cancer sufferers.

WORK

1 a Why do you think many Britons were proud of their nation in 1900?

b For what reasons might some Britons have been worried about their nation's status by 1900?

2 Look at **Source B**.

a Write a sentence or two describing each of the photographs.

b What details in the photographs helped you to decide which area was rich and which was poor?

c Do you think **Source C** is describing the rich area or the poor one? Explain how you made your decision.

3 a Design a poster that describes Britain at the start of the twentieth century. Your poster should:

• be aimed at a Year 6 pupil who has never studied Britain in the early 1900s;

• include <u>no more</u> than 50 words;

• mention the rich/poor divide, the position of women, shopping, the media, sport and transport developments.

b Using the same guidelines, design another poster that describes Britain at the start of the twenty-first century (the year 2000).

c In what areas and categories are the two posters similar and how are they different?

Why do we have school dinners?

▸ How healthy were Britain's children at the start of the twentieth century?
▸ How did the Government help them?

Today, a hot, nutritious school dinner is available for every schoolchild in Britain. But why do we have school dinners? When did this tradition start? And what were some of the early school dinners like?

In 1902, Charles Booth published his final report on *Life and Labour of the People of London*. He discovered that nearly one-third of all Londoners were so poor that they didn't have enough money to eat properly, despite having full-time jobs. The problems weren't just in London. At around the same time, up in York, Seebohm Rowntree (of the sweet family) found that 43% of the city's wage earners were not earning enough to live on.

▾ **Source A** Taken from an interview in 'Poverty: A Study of Town Life', by S Rowntree, 1901.

'If there's anything extra to buy, such as a pair of boots for one of the children, me and the children go without dinner — or maybe only 'as a cuppa tea and a bit of bread, but Jack 'ollers [shouts] to take his dinner to work and I give it to 'im as usual. He never knows we go without and I never tells 'im.'

These two investigations caused quite a stir – and famous politicians like David Lloyd George and a young Winston Churchill felt that governments should try harder to look after people who couldn't help themselves. Army leaders soon became worried too. Nearly one-third of all men who volunteered to join the army failed their medical examination because they were too small, too thin, too ill or had poor eyesight. Unless something was done about the health of the nation's young men, how was Britain going to fight its wars in the future?

Amongst the hardest hit were children. Millions of youngsters were not getting the good diet they needed because their parents couldn't afford enough food and

didn't know enough about healthy eating. And calling a doctor cost money in the early 1900s, so parents rarely did unless they were desperate!

Despite great efforts in the 1800s to improve living and working conditions, by 1900, 15 children out of every 100 were still dying before their fifth birthday. Also, a poor child was, on average, 9cm shorter than a rich one!

In 1906, the general election was won by the Liberal Party. They were committed to trying to wipe out poverty … and decided to start with children. One of the first moves they made was to introduce free school meals for the poorest children.

▾ **Source B** A typical week of free school meals. The poorest children could eat for free, but other children could buy a meal for a small charge. By 1914, over 158 000 children were having free meals once a day, every day.

THIS WEEK'S MENU

Monday: Tomato soup ~ Currant roly-poly pudding

Tuesday: Meat pudding ~ Rice pudding

Wednesday: Yorkshire pudding, gravy, peas ~ Rice pudding and sultanas

Thursday: Vegetable soup ~ Currant pastry or fruit tart

Friday: Stewed fish, parsley sauce, peas, mashed potatoes ~ Blancmange

Other measures were introduced too – free medical checks and free medical treatment for example. They even introduced a Children's Charter, which laid down in law many of the things that still protect young people today.

▼ **Source C** Children's Charter (or the Children's Act, 1908). As you can see, many of these reforms are still in place today.

- Children are 'protected persons' – parents can be prosecuted if they neglect or are cruel to them.
- Inspectors to regularly visit any children who have been neglected in the past.
- All children's homes to be regularly inspected.
- Youth courts and young offenders' homes set up to keep young criminals away from older ones.
- Children under 14 not allowed in pubs.
- Shopkeepers cannot sell cigarettes to children under 16.

▼ **Source D** An anxious mother watches the doctor examine her son in one of Britain's first free medical checks.

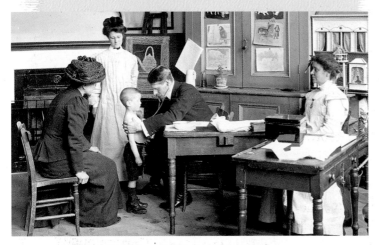

After helping children, the new Liberal Government moved on to help other vulnerable sections of society. They introduced unemployment benefit (the 'dole'), sickness benefit and old age pensions. They even built Britain's first job centres.

▼ **Source E** This graph shows how children gained (and lost) weight during part of the year.

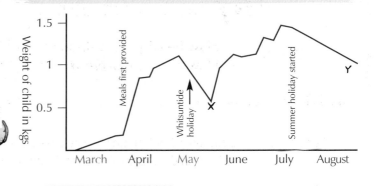

FACT: ▶ A new party

▶ In Victorian times, there were two main political parties – the Conservatives and the Liberals. In the 1890s, a new political party was formed – the Labour Party. Some say the Liberal Party's attempts to help ordinary, working people and children after 1906 was an attempt to pull voters away from the new Labour Party!

WORK

1 a Who were i) Charles Booth and ii) Seebohm Rowntree?
  b Why do you think their reports shocked so many people?

2 Why do you think army leaders were so worried about the health of Britain's young men in 1900?

3 Look at **Source B**.
  a Why were school meals introduced?
  b Choose any day from the source and write a few sentences comparing it to the meal you ate for dinner on the same day. You might wish to make a judgement about which was the healthier meal – yours or the one a young person would have had in 1906.

4 Look at **Source E**.
  a Draw **Source E** in your book. Remember to label it carefully.
  b What was the result of introducing school meals? Try to use figures in your answer.
  c Why did children lose weight in May and July?

5 a Apart from the introduction of school meals, how else were children helped in the early 1900s?
  b Why do you think that helping children was seen as one of the main priorities by the new Liberal Government?

9

Titanic tour

▸ What was the *Titanic* like?
▸ Were rich and poor treated equally?

The sinking of the *Titanic* on its **maiden voyage** is one of the worst – and certainly most famous – shipping disasters of all time. Built at a cost of £1.5 million (it would cost £222 million to build today) in Belfast for the White Star Shipping Line, it weighed 46 000 tons and was the length of three football pitches. *Titanic* was as high as a 17 storey building!

The owners said that the *Titanic* was 'practically unsinkable' because its **hull** consisted of 16 watertight compartments – and four could be flooded at one time without the ship going down. The owners also advertised luxurious first-class accommodation, a state-of-the-art gymnasium, a swimming pool, a tennis court and a Parisian cafe. One top-of-the-range voyage from Southampton to New York could cost £870 – that's £27 000 today!

Titanic's first voyage began in Southampton at midday on Wednesday 10 April 1912. The ship called at Cherbourg in France and Queenstown in Southern Ireland, before heading out across the Atlantic Ocean towards New York. On board were some of the richest and poorest people in the world. For the richer passengers (there were 322 in first class), it was a chance to say they had taken a trip on the world's largest luxury liner. For the poorer people (there were 709 in third class), this was their chance for a new life in America. Poor British passengers were joined by Russians, Italians, Swedes, Germans, Spaniards, French and many other nationalities in the basic third-class compartments deep down in the ship. Some had paid as little as £3 (£95 today) for their treasured ticket.

Now it's your chance to go on a tour of one of the world's most famous ships.

▾ **Source A** A photograph of *Titanic's* anchor, pictured here on its way to Belfast from where it was made in Netherton, West Midlands.

▾ **Source B** The original plans for the *Titanic*. Note how many lifeboats were originally designed to be on board.

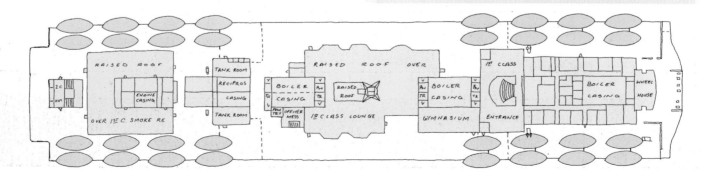

Source C A first-class bedroom

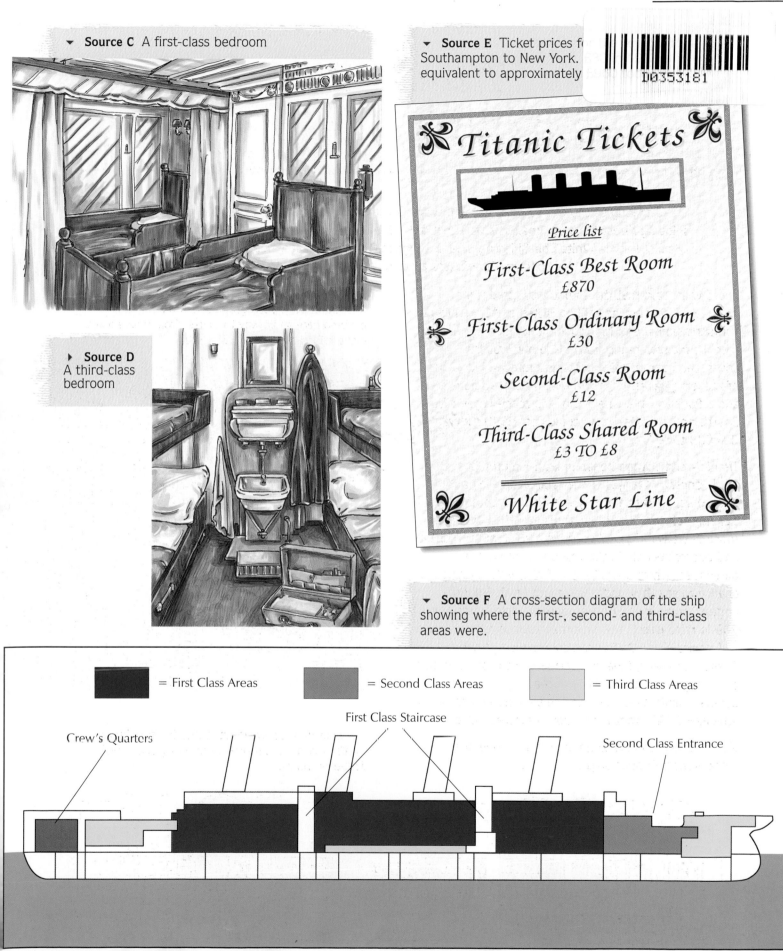

Source E Ticket prices f[...]
Southampton to New York.
equivalent to approximately [...]

D0353181

Titanic Tickets

Price list

First-Class Best Room
£870

First-Class Ordinary Room
£30

Second-Class Room
£12

Third-Class Shared Room
£3 TO £8

White Star Line

Source D
A third-class
bedroom

Source F A cross-section diagram of the ship showing where the first-, second- and third-class areas were.

= First Class Areas   = Second Class Areas   = Third Class Areas

First Class Staircase

Crew's Quarters

Second Class Entrance

WHITE STAR LINE
ROYAL STEAMERS
UNITED STATES MAIL

FIRST SAILING OF THE LATEST ADDITION TO THE WHITE STAR FLEET

The Queen of the Ocean

TITANIC

LENGTH 882 FT   OVER 45,000 TONS   BEAM 92 FT
TRIPLE-SCREWS

WHITE STAR LINE PIER 59 North River, NEW YORK

Saturday, April 20th At 12 Noon

THIRD CLASS RATES ARE:

To PLYMOUTH, SOUTHAMPTON, LONDON, LIVERPOOL and GLASGOW: $36.25
To GOTHENBURG, MALMO, CHRISTIANIA, COPENHAGEN, ESBERG, Etc. 41.50
To STOCKHOLM, ÅBO, HANGO, HELSINGFORS: 44.50
To HAMBURG, BREMEN, ANTWERP, AMSTERDAM, ROTTERDAM, HAVRE, CHERBOURG: 45.00

WHITE STAR LINE, 9 Broadway, New York

TICKETS FOR SALE HERE

▲ **Source H** A poster, put up around New York, advertising the *return* voyage from New York to Southampton – a trip that would never take place!

TITANIC MENU

First-class Dinner Menu
14 April 1912

Hors d'oeuvres • Salmon and cucumber
• Cream of barley soup

Sirloin steak with potatoes • Roast chicken and vegetable rice
• Lamb and mint sauce • Duck and apple sauce

Green peas • New potatoes • Roast potatoes • Carrots • Rice
• Asparagus vinaigrette • Celery

Chocolate éclairs • Peaches and cream • French ice cream

▲ **Source I** The first-class dinner menu for Sunday 14 April 1912. For many, this would be the last meal of their lives!

▼ **Source G** *Titanic* left Southampton on Wednesday 10 April 1912. However, just moments after leaving the dock at Southampton, it nearly collided with another ship!

◄ **Source J** A picture of the first-class dining area

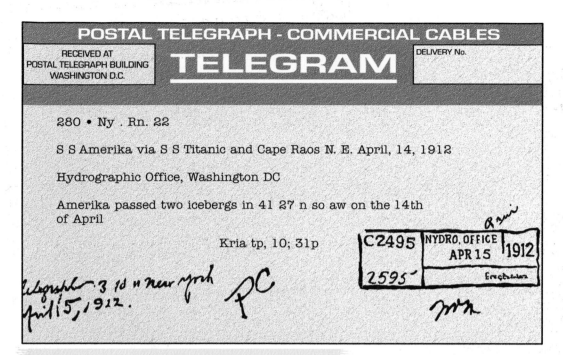

POSTAL TELEGRAPH - COMMERCIAL CABLES
TELEGRAM

RECEIVED AT
POSTAL TELEGRAPH BUILDING
WASHINGTON D.C.

DELIVERY No.

280 • Ny . Rn. 22

S S Amerika via S S Titanic and Cape Raos N. E. April, 14, 1912

Hydrographic Office, Washington DC

Amerika passed two icebergs in 41 27 n so aw on the 14th
of April

Kria tp, 10; 31p

C2495 NYDRO. OFFICE
APR 15 1912

2595

▲ **Source K** An ice warning, issued at 1:45pm by
Amerika, a ship nearby

▼ **Source L** The ship's captain, E J Smith, said
this in an interview in 1910. The captain was a
very well respected sailor who'd had a successful
and accident-free career.

'When anyone asks me to describe my career at
sea, I just say – uneventful. Of course there
have been winter gales, storms and fog, but in
all my years, I have never been in an accident.
I've only seen one ship in trouble in all my
years at sea. I've never seen a wreck, have
never been wrecked, and I have never been in a
situation that threatened to end in disaster.'

On the evening of Sunday 14 April, out in the middle of the Atlantic Ocean, the temperature dropped below freezing and the chance of striking an iceberg became a very real danger. Just before midnight, the lookouts saw the shadowy outline of an iceberg 'dead ahead'. Despite turning to try to avoid it, *Titanic* struck the iceberg and was holed below the waterline.

The emergency doors were closed and the engines were stopped. However, five of the sixteen watertight compartments had been gashed open – water was pouring in. The ship could only withstand up to four compartments being flooded without sinking! Less than three hours later, *Titanic* sank. Tragically, only 704 people were rescued from over 2 200 on board.

> **(!) WISE UP WORDS**
>
> hull   maiden voyage

WORK

You can work in groups of two or three for this task, although it can be done individually.

1 Your team has been specially selected by the White Star Line to mount an advertising campaign that promotes the *Titanic's* maiden voyage. They hope your efforts will fill their ship to capacity. They want:

   • a smart, well designed leaflet or brochure that boasts the luxurious facilities, speed, size and status of the world's most famous ship. This leaflet could be sent to some of the wealthiest people in the land.

   • a poster (or two) that aims to attract third-class passengers looking for a new life in America. Their needs may be slightly different to other, richer passengers – they want cheap tickets, a warm bed and a safe, quick journey – so you must plan your poster accordingly.

   • a radio advertisement – no more than one minute long. Make it fun and interesting, perhaps using some of today's advertisements for inspiration.

2 Write a paragraph explaining how and why your leaflet and poster are different.

HISTORY MYSTERY

Why did Titanic sink?

'We have struck an iceberg … sinking fast … come to our assistance … cannot last much longer.'

The sinking of the *Titanic*, with the loss of over 1 500 lives, caused uproar on both sides of the Atlantic. Like most disasters, people looked around for someone, or something, to blame.

Now it's time for you to turn into a History Mystery detective. Imagine you are put in charge of investigating the tragedy. Your inquiry must evaluate all the evidence. Write a report for the US and British governments. Your report should be entitled – 'Why did *Titanic* sink?' Best of luck!

EVIDENCE A

Was it Captain Smith's fault?

Captain Smith was due to retire after *Titanic*'s maiden voyage. Did he want to retire from sailing by getting to New York in record time? He ignored at least seven ice warnings from other ships nearby. Despite having men on the lookout for icebergs, *Titanic* was still travelling at 20 knots per hour, close to its top speed. If the ship was going slower, maybe it could have turned out of the iceberg's way in time! Perhaps Captain Smith thought that an iceberg couldn't sink a modern ship. He once said, 'I can't imagine anything causing a ship to founder [sink]. Modern shipbuilding has gone beyond that.'

EVIDENCE C

Was it Thomas Andrews' fault?

Thomas Andrews designed the ship. Many thought *Titanic* was unsinkable because it had 16 watertight compartments and as many as four could let in water before the ship would sink. However, the compartments didn't reach as high as they should have done. Mr Andrews reduced their height to make more space in some of the first-class rooms. If two watertight compartments reached all the way up to the top of the ship, maybe *Titanic* wouldn't have sunk.

EVIDENCE B

Was it the shipbuilder's fault?

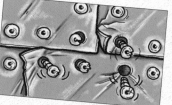

Titanic was built at Harland and Wolff Shipyard in Belfast, Ireland. About three million rivets were used to hold the ship together. When the wreck of *Titanic* was found on the ocean floor in 1985, some of the rivets were brought back up to the surface and analysed. Investigations showed that the rivets were made of poor-quality iron. When the side of the ship hit the iceberg, the heads of the rivets broke off and sections of the ship came apart. If the rivets were made of better quality iron, perhaps the sections of the ship may have stayed together – perhaps the ship would not have sunk at all! Further tests on steel used for the hull showed that it became **brittle** in extremely cold conditions – such as on the night of 14 April!

EVIDENCE D

Was it Captain Lord's fault?

Walter Lord captained the *Californian*, a ship only 19 miles away from *Titanic* when it struck the iceberg. It was the *Californian* that sent the *Titanic* its final ice warning.

At around 11:15pm, the *Californian's* radio operator went to bed. After midnight, the crew saw rockets being fired into the sky on the horizon. Captain Lord was woken up but decided not to sail towards the fireworks – he thought the ship (which he later realised was the *Titanic*) was just having a party! Should the *Californian* have investigated the rockets? Should Captain Lord have at least turned on the radio? He would then have heard the distress messages and would have been able to help.

EVIDENCE E

Was it Bruce Ismay's fault?

Bruce Ismay was in charge of the White Star Line, the owners of *Titanic*. He was travelling on board ship but managed to get into a lifeboat as the ship went down. Ismay wanted to prove that the White Star Line was better than all other shipping companies. Did he put pressure on Captain Smith to make the ship go as fast as it could, despite travelling through a sea of icebergs? Was he hoping to get *Titanic* to make a record crossing? One witness, who survived the sinking, claimed she heard Ismay and Smith arguing on Saturday 13 April!

Also, was Ismay responsible for more deaths than there should have been? If you look on the original plans (**Source B**, p10), *Titanic* was originally designed to have 32 lifeboats. The finished ship only had 20 – enough for only 1 178 of the 2 206 on board. The White Star Line had some of the lifeboats removed to make more room for first-class passengers!

(!) WISE UP WORD

brittle

WORK

So who was to blame for the sinking of the *Titanic*? It's time to be a History Mystery detective. Start to formulate your theory.

Step 1 Analyse the evidence.

Under the following headings, write a sentence or two outlining how each may have contributed to the sinking.
i) Captain Smith ii) The shipbuilders iii) Thomas Andrews iv) Captain Lord v) Bruce Ismay.

Step 2 Prioritise the evidence.

In your opinion, is one person more at fault than any other? Can you put your list in order of responsibility? Did one person's actions contribute more to the sinking than any others? Write a paragraph or two explaining why you made your decision. Did some people have nothing at all to do

with the sinking? If so, say who and how you arrived at this conclusion.

Step 3 Deliver your verdict.

Time to write up your report and present your findings:

- start your report with a brief introduction to the disaster;
- outline the role in the sinking of each person under investigation;
- write a conclusion – is one person to blame or several, or a combination of all?
- Remember, if you don't blame <u>one</u> person, it doesn't mean your investigation has failed! There is often more than one factor to consider in most investigations.

What can the *Titanic* tell us?

▸ What do the casualty figures tell us about class attitudes?
▸ What changes took place as a result of the disaster?

When it was built, *Titanic* was the most luxurious ship ever produced. Posters all over Britain advertised the quality of the first-class accommodation. However, there were only 322 first-class passengers on board. There were 277 in second class, yet the vast majority of passengers travelled in the third-class accommodation.

A third-class ticket meant a bunk bed in a shared room, basic food, basic toilets and cramped conditions. There was no wallpaper on the walls and no carpets on the floor. Even walking about on the top deck was strictly 'out of bounds' for the third-class travellers. Yet the White Star Line, and other shipping companies, made vast sums of money from these poorer passengers. Most had saved for a long time to get enough money to start a new life in America. The White Star Line transported thousands and thousands to the 'land of opportunity'. In fact, between 1900 and 1910, about 11 million Europeans crossed the Atlantic to settle in the USA. Over three million of them were British.

So what were a third-class passenger's chances of survival on the sinking *Titanic*? Who stood the best chance of getting a place on a lifeboat? And what does the *Titanic's* casualty list tell us about attitudes at the time?

▸ **Source A** Passengers on other ships described seeing an iceberg with a smear of red paint running along the base. This is the type of mark *Titanic* would have left on the iceberg it hit.

▲ Early reports said that the Titanic had been damaged but would arrive in New York with all its passengers safely on board. This newspaper headline revealed the terrible truth!

▼ **Source B** Timeline of disaster

Sunday 14 April

10:55pm *Titanic* receives ninth ice warning of the day from nearby ship, the *Californian*. *Titanic's* telegraph operator tells them to 'shut up'!

11:30pm Telegraph operation on the *Californian* signs off for the night and goes to bed.

11:40pm *Titanic* lookouts spot iceberg. Seconds later, the ship hits iceberg.

Monday 15 April

Midnight Captain Smith and Thomas Andrews (designer) inspect the damage. Andrews thinks *Titanic* will sink in two hours. Smith has distress calls sent to any nearby ships.

12:05am Captain Smith orders passengers to put on their lifebelts. Also orders that lifeboats be readied. If fully loaded, the lifeboats could carry 1 178 people – there were 2 206 on board.

12:15am *Titanic's* band begins to play lively music to help prevent a panic.

12:25am The lifeboats begin to be loaded with women and children.

12:45am First lifeboat – lifeboat 7 – is lowered into the water. It holds 28 passengers, but can carry 65. Many passengers preferred to stay on the ship.

12:55am Lifeboat 7 leaves. Lifeboat 5 (not full) soon follows.

1:00am Lifeboats 3 and 11 leave.

1:10am Lifeboat 1 leaves. Only 12 passengers are on board; it can hold 40.

1:20am Lifeboat 9 leaves (not full).

1:25am Lifeboats 12 and 8 leave.

1:30am Lifeboats 14 and 16 leave.

1:35am Lifeboats 13 and 10 leave.

1:40am Collapsible boat C leaves with Bruce Ismay (in charge of White Star Line) on board. He is later criticised for this.

1:45am Lifeboats 2 and 6 leave.

1:55am Lifeboats 4 and 15 leave.

2:05am Collapsible boat D leaves.

2:17am Crew told to save themselves. Collapsible boats A and B are washed overboard. Passengers cling to them.

2:20am *Titanic* sinks.

4:10am Nearby ship, the *Carpathia*, begins to pick up survivors.

▼ **Source C** Casualty figures issued shortly after the sinking

First class

	On board	Rescued	% Rescued
Men	173	58	34
Women	144	139	97
Children	5	5	100
Total	**322**	**202**	**63**

Second class

	On board	Rescued	% Rescued
Men	160	13	8
Women	93	78	84
Children	24	24	100
Total	**277**	**115**	**42**

Third class

	On board	Rescued	% Rescued
Men	454	55	12
Women	179	98	55
Children	76	23	30
Total	**709**	**176**	**25**

Total passengers and crew

	On board	Rescued	% Rescued
Men	1 662	315	19
Women	439	338	77
Children	105	51	49
Total	**2 206**	**704**	**32**

Source D A photograph of some rescued first-class passengers. They are still dressed in their evening suits and dresses.

▶ **Source E** Signs like this appeared all over the ship. **Steerage** was another word for third-class passengers. During the voyage, they were prevented from going near the first-class areas. Some survivors said that doors were locked to prevent them going into first-class areas even after the ship had struck the iceberg. Another survivor commented, 'I only realised that the situation was serious when I saw some steerage passengers in the first-class area!'

The Titanic disaster shocked the world. It happened at a time when many people were beginning to think that anything was possible. The motor car and the aeroplane were very recent inventions and many thought that anything could be achieved through the application of science and technology. However, a simple iceberg sank the greatest ship ever built. Man had been beaten by nature. More shocking to others was the fact that only 25% of third-class passengers survived. To many, it seemed that their lives were worth much less than a first-class traveller – 63% of first-class passengers survived!

Major changes took place after the *Titanic* disaster. After 1913, all ships had to have:

- regular lifeboat drills
- lifeboat places for *everyone* on board
- a radio operated 24 hours a day

Also, it was recommended that all ships should reduce their speed in ice, fog or any other areas of possible danger.

FACT: ▶ Predicting a disaster

▶ In 1898, a writer named Morgan Robertson wrote a book about a ship called *Titan*. In the book, Robertson writes that *Titan* was 'the largest craft afloat' and 'was considered practically unsinkable'. However, *Titan* hits an iceberg in the Atlantic Ocean on its first voyage. This ship doesn't have enough lifeboats and many of its passengers die!

▼ **Source F** A survivor comments on the disaster

'I only realised that the situation was serious when I saw a third-class passenger on the first-class deck.'

! WISE UP WORD

steerage

WORK

1 a Explain what is meant by the word 'steerage'.
   b Why do you think so many steerage passengers bought tickets on *Titanic*?

2 Look at **Source B**.
   a Why do you think *Titanic* ignored so many ice warnings?
   b Why were there not enough lifeboat places for everyone on board? You might need to look back to page 15 to help with your answer.
   c Why do you think the first few lifeboats that left *Titanic* were not full?
   d Why did *Titanic's* band begin to play lively music despite the fact that the ship was sinking?

3 Look at **Source C**.
   a Make a copy of the source in your book.
   b What percentages of first- and second-class children were rescued?
   c What percentage of third-class children were rescued?
   d What percentage of first-class men were rescued?
   e Do your answers to C and D mean that the order 'women and children first' was correctly followed?
   f Which class of passengers suffered the most?
   g What does this evidence tell you about class attitudes to the rich and poor at the time?

Why did the Great War start?

AIMS
- ▸ What were the main causes of the Great War?
- ▸ How exactly did it start?

You can go to almost any town or village in Britain and see the names of dead soldiers, sailors and aircrew carved on stone memorials like the one in **Source A**. Is there one near to your home or in your town or village?

◂ **Source A** This is a memorial to the 61 ex-pupils of Castle High School, Dudley, who died during the Great War of 1914–1918. It is outside the school's library. The memorial also includes the name of a teacher who joined up to fight in September 1914. He was killed in action in France two years later, aged 31. One man, an 18 year old called Clifford Cox, left the school in July 1915, joined the army soon after and was declared 'missing, feared killed in action' only 12 months later. His body was never found.

HUNGRY FOR MORE?

Where is the nearest Great War memorial to you?

Why not go and visit it? You could draw a picture or take a photograph of it.

Copy out some of the names and research their deaths on www.cwgc.org.uk – the official website of the burial grounds for each Great War soldier who died whilst fighting.

The Great War wasn't 'great' because men had an enjoyable adventure and a great time. It was called the Great War because a war so big had never taken place before. Millions and millions of men, divided into two sides or **alliances**, spent over four years trying to kill each other. They used some of the most sophisticated weapons the world had ever seen. In total, nearly nine million people were killed – that's over 5 000 deaths *per day* for over four years! Some people even called it 'the war to end all wars'. They thought it was so bad that men would never again allow themselves to be drawn into such a horrific war.

So how did this Great War start? What caused it in the first place? Why did so many people join up to fight?

Wars start because countries cannot solve their problems by talking. However, wars are rarely started by people like Clifford Cox, or by other ordinary people like those sitting in your classroom or living in your street. Wars are usually started by politicians, by kings and by queens.

The Great War started because people in power from several different countries could not sort out their disagreements properly. By 1914, some of the leaders of the most powerful countries in Europe had been arguing for years. They argued about what bits of land they owned and what bits of land they wanted. They even argued about who was allowed to have the biggest army and navy.

By 1914, some of the most powerful countries in Europe had formed themselves into two rival gangs, or alliances as they were known. One group was known as the **Triple Alliance** and contained leaders from Germany, Austria-Hungary and Italy. The other group was called the **Triple Entente** and contained leaders from Britain, France and Russia. Each country was powerful and well armed. If a quarrel started between just two of them, it was certain that the quarrel would quickly spread as they called on their **allies** to help.

▼ **Source B** From the Castle High School newsletter, Christmas Edition, 1916

'It is our sad duty to report that Clifford Cox, who joined up as soon as he was old enough, is missing after a ferocious battle with German troops near the River Somme, France, on 23 July 1916.'

▼ **Source C** How the countries lined up for war

HOW THE SIDES LINED UP FOR THE GREAT WAR

GREAT BRITAIN

London

BELGIUM

GERMANY

Berlin

RUSSIA

Moscow

FRANCE

Paris

Vienna

AUSTRIA-HUNGARY

ITALY

Rome

TRIPLE ALLIANCE
Germany
Austria-Hungary
Italy

versus

TRIPLE ENTENTE
France
Russia
Great Britain

But how exactly did war break out?

How did one man start a chain reaction that ended with the largest war the world had ever seen? And how did the pre-war alliances contribute to the start of the war?

In June 1914, Europe was close to war. In fact, it seemed as if some of the leaders in the Triple Alliance and the Triple Entente were *desperate* to try out their war plans and new weapons. All that was needed was a spark to make the whole of Europe explode into war. On 28 June 1914, the 'spark' arrived!

On 28 June 1914, Archduke Franz Ferdinand, an Austrian prince, arrived in Sarajevo with his wife, Sophie. Sarajevo was the capital city of Bosnia, a region which Austria-Hungary had conquered in 1908. Franz Josef, King of Austria-Hungary, was proud of his empire – sending his nephew, Franz, to Sarajevo on a visit was a way of letting his people know this!

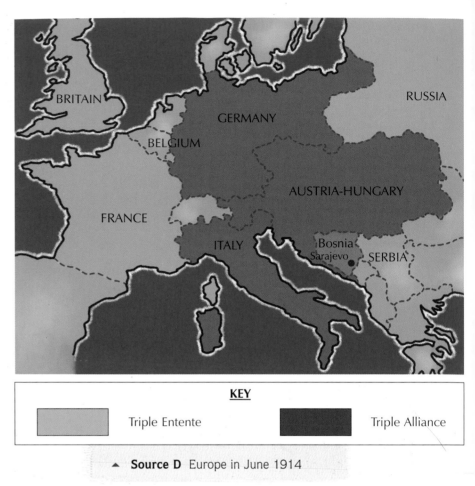

KEY		
	Triple Entente		Triple Alliance

▲ **Source D** Europe in June 1914

▼ **Source E** Which side looks most powerful in 1914 – the Triple Alliance or the Triple Entente?

Country	Population (millions)	Population of overseas colonies (millions)	Size of army (millions of soldiers)	Size of navy
Germany	63	15	4.2	281 ships
Austria-Hungary	50	–	0.8	67 ships
Italy	35	2	0.7	36 ships
Britain	41	390	0.7	388 ships
France	40	63	3.7	207 ships
Russia	139	–	1.2	166 ships

Many Bosnians didn't want to be part of Austria-Hungary at all. They wanted to join with their neighbours, Serbia, instead. Many Serbians wanted to join with Bosnia too. One gang of Serbians, led by a student called Gavrilo Princip, decided to take drastic action and strike a terrible blow to the country they hated ... they would kill Archduke Ferdinand, next in line to the Austro-Hungarian throne. On 28 June 1914, they would get their chance.

Archduke Franz Ferdinand arrived at Sarajevo Station at 9:28am. It was his wedding anniversary. As his car made its way to the town hall for a meeting with the mayor, Gavrilo Princip and five of his mates were waiting. As he slowly passed by, one of Gavrilo's gang threw a bomb at the Archduke's car. The Archduke caught the bomb and threw it on the floor. It blew up under the car behind, injuring eight people. The Archduke's car sped off to the town hall with the Archduke in a furious mood. He cancelled the rest of the visit. The bomb-thrower swallowed poison and jumped into a river.

▲ **Source F** A drawing of the assassination, published on 12 July 1914.

At 11:00am, the Archduke and his wife left the town hall in their chauffeur-driven car. They were going to visit the people injured by the bomb. The car was travelling a lot faster this time! However, the driver took the wrong road and stopped to turn around. As the Archduke looked around to see if all was clear, he came face-to-face with Gavrilo Princip.

> **WISE UP WORDS**
>
> Triple Alliance   Triple Entente   alliance   allies

Princip fired two shots. The first hit the Archduke in the throat. The second hit Sophie in the stomach. They both died. It was 11:30am. Princip swallowed poison but it failed to work. He was arrested and beaten up.

WORK

1 Write a sentence or two to explain the following words:
   alliance • allies

2 Look at **Source C**.
   a Make a list of the countries in i) the Triple Alliance ii) the Triple Entente.
   b If the Triple Alliance attacked France, how could Russia's friendship help France?
   c If Austria-Hungary attacked Russia, how could France's friendship help Russia?

   d If Russia attacked Germany, how could Austria-Hungary's friendship help Germany?
   e The various alliances have been described as 'two sets of mountain climbers roped together'. What are the advantages and disadvantages of being 'roped together'?

3 Look at **Source E**.
   a Why do you think i) Britain had a bigger navy than other countries and ii) a smaller army?
   b In your opinion, which alliance was stronger in 1914? Give reasons for your answer.

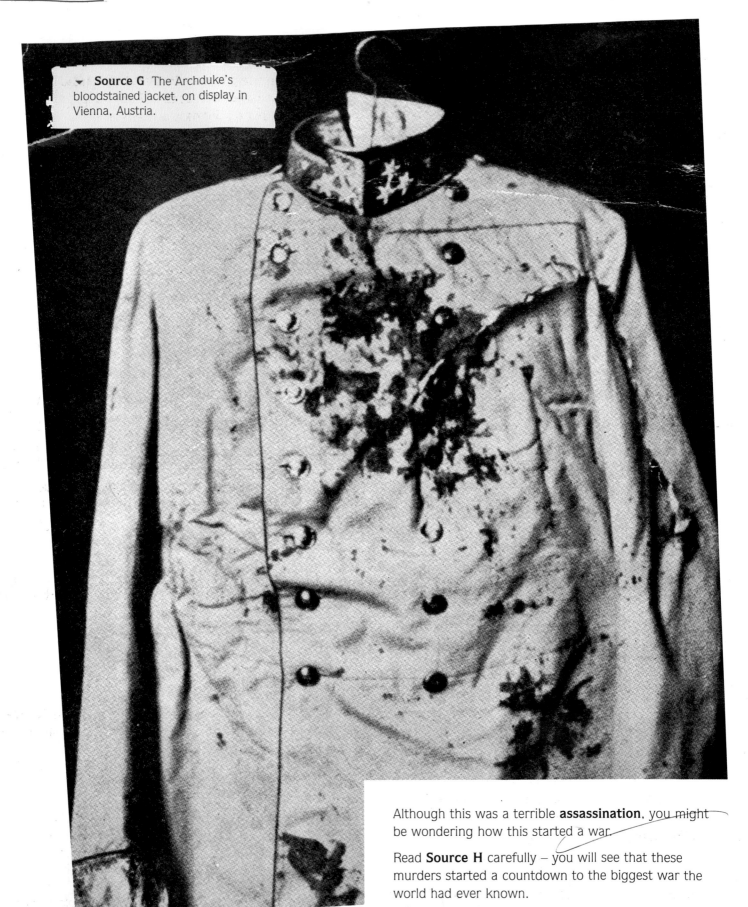

Source G The Archduke's bloodstained jacket, on display in Vienna, Austria.

Although this was a terrible **assassination**, you might be wondering how this started a war.

Read **Source H** carefully – you will see that these murders started a countdown to the biggest war the world had ever known.

▼ **Source H** Timeline of events

28 July: Austria-Hungary blames Serbia for killing their Archduke. They attack Serbia.

29 July: Russia, who has promised to protect Serbia against attack, gets its army ready to attack Austria-Hungary.

1 August: Germany, who supports Austria-Hungary, hears about Russian preparations for war. Germany declares war on Russia.

2 August: Britain prepares its warships.

3 August: Germany, whose plan is to defeat France BEFORE attacking Russia, declares war on France.

4 August: Germany asks Belgium to allow German soldiers to march through their country to attack France. Belgium says 'no'. Germany marches in anyway. Britain, who has a deal to protect Belgium from attack (dating back to 1839), declares war on Germany.

6 August: Austria-Hungary declares war on Russia.

12 August: Britain and France declare war on Austria-Hungary.

As **Source H** shows, the murders in Sarajevo on that Sunday morning in June 1914 started a whole chain of events that threw Europe into war, a war in which millions of people would die.

FACT: ▶ The final line-up

▶ Italy didn't join straight away. Instead, they waited until 1915 and joined in on Britain, France and Russia's side – not on Germany and Austria-Hungary's side as promised in the Triple Alliance. Although 28 countries joined in total, the major countries fought on these sides.

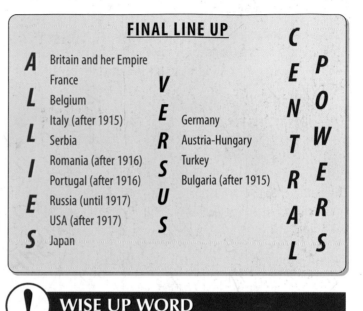

FINAL LINE UP

A L L I E S

Britain and her Empire
France
Belgium
Italy (after 1915)
Serbia
Romania (after 1916)
Portugal (after 1916)
Russia (until 1917)
USA (after 1917)
Japan

V E R S U S

Germany
Austria-Hungary
Turkey
Bulgaria (after 1915)

C E N T R A L   P O W E R S

(!) **WISE UP WORD**

assassination

WORK

1   Match up the names on the left with the correct description on the right.

Archduke Franz Ferdinand	The capital city of Bosnia, the place where Franz Ferdinand visited on 28 June 1914.
Sarajevo	A large, powerful country that ruled an area called Bosnia. Many Bosnians hated this and wanted to join with Serbia.
Gavrilo Princip	Next in line to the Austro-Hungarian throne.
Austria-Hungary	An independent country. Many Serbians wanted Bosnia to unite with their country.
Serbia	A Serbian student, part of a gang who wanted to kill Franz Ferdinand.

2   Prepare an 'on the spot' newspaper report on the assassination of Franz Ferdinand. Include:

• an eye-catching headline;
• details of the main events;
• eyewitness accounts, if possible;
• a picture from the scene.

Note: Some of you may wish to do it from the Austro-Hungarian point of view, whilst others may wish to write it as a Serbian news reporter.

3   Look at **Source H**. Why did:

a   Austria-Hungary attack Serbia?
b   Russia attack Austria-Hungary?
c   Germany support Austria-Hungary?
d   Germany invade Belgium?
e   Britain declare war on Germany?

4   Did Gavrilo Princip start the Great War? Explain your answer carefully – you may want to discuss it and/or plan your answer as a class first.

Joining up

AIMS
▶ Why did men choose to fight?
▶ How did the Government use propaganda to attract more volunteers?

Britain joined the war on 4 August 1914. At once, the Government asked for volunteers aged between 19 and 30 to come forward to join the army. To begin with, there was a great rush to join up. A wave of **patriotism** swept over the country as men decided to 'do their bit for King and country'. One million men had enlisted by December 1914, keen to get involved in a war they thought might be over by Christmas. Few realised what they were letting themselves in for!

The Government worked hard to keep a constant stream of volunteers queuing up at their local **recruitment** office. 'Go to war with your pals' was the message as they promised to keep friends together who joined up at the same time. As a result, whole football teams, orchestras, bus depots and old school friends signed up with each other.

A huge **propaganda** campaign was started throughout the country. Leaflets and posters were issued that tried to persuade men to join up. They always made the British soldier look like a hero, whilst any Germans looked like cruel savages! News of battle victories filled the newspapers, whilst defeats were hardly mentioned. Even women were encouraged to get their boyfriends or husbands to join in. Some women went as far as to hand out white feathers, a mark of a coward, to any men they thought should be in the army! This propaganda campaign was very successful – by January 1916, about 2.5 million men had agreed to fight.

▶ **Source B**
This poster shows a German nurse pouring water on the floor in front of a thirsty, injured British soldier. Two fat Germans laugh in the background. How do you think this made some British men feel?

RED CROSS OR IRON CROSS?

WOUNDED AND A PRISONER OUR SOLDIER CRIES FOR WATER.
THE GERMAN "SISTER"
POURS IT ON THE GROUND BEFORE HIS EYES.
·THERE IS NO WOMAN IN BRITAIN WHO WOULD DO IT.
THERE IS NO WOMAN IN BRITAIN WHO WILL FORGET IT.

▶ **Source A** One of the most famous recruitment posters of all time. It shows Earl Kitchener, the man in charge of getting enough men to fight, asking for volunteers to join the army. By a clever new technique, wherever you stand, Kitchener always seems to be staring and pointing directly at YOU.

BRITONS
"WANTS"
YOU
JOIN YOUR COUNTRY'S ARMY!
GOD SAVE THE KING
Reproduced by permission of LONDON OPINION

▶ **Source C**
What did the designer of this poster hope young women would go and do after they had read it?

TO THE YOUNG WOMEN OF LONDON

Is your "Best Boy" wearing Khaki? If not don't **YOU THINK** he should be?

If he does not think that you and your country are worth fighting for—do you think he is **WORTHY** of you?

Don't pity the girl who is alone—her young man is probably a soldier—fighting for her and her country—and for **YOU**.

If your young man neglects his duty to his King and Country, the time may come when he will **NEGLECT YOU**.

Think it over—then ask him to

JOIN THE ARMY TO-DAY

Source D This is a very clever poster based on the original. Why do you think the father looks so upset or guilty?

Daddy, what did YOU do in the Great War?

Source E Part of a letter written by a young soldier to his mum, Christmas 1914. A 'gong' is a nickname for a medal.

'I hate the thought of missing out. It's my chance to do something, you know, to contribute to the war effort. I might even get a gong if I'm lucky ... and the girls; they love a man in uniform, don't they?'

Source F George Coppard, in his book *With a Machine-gun to Cambrai*, tells how he lied about his age to join. He was really 16 years old. One boy, Valentine Strudwick, joined up when he was 13! He was killed by a German bomb one year later.

'The sergeant asked me my age and when told, replied, "Clear off, son, come back tomorrow and we'll see if you're nineteen, eh?" So I turned up the next day and gave my age as nineteen ... holding up my right hand I swore to fight for King and country. The sergeant winked as he gave me the King's shilling.'

[A shilling was worth 5p. Accepting it was a sign that you had agreed to join the army.]

By the summer of 1916, the flood of volunteers had begun to slow down. People were beginning to realise that the war was not such a big adventure; men were dying or returning home wounded and crippled for life. The Government's solution was to introduce **conscription**. This meant that any man, aged between 18 and 41, could be *forced* to join the army. Some refused to join when the letter dropped through the letterbox, but by April 1918, an extra 2.5 million men had been found through conscription.

FACT: ▶ 'Conshies'

▶ Some men believed that war was wrong and wouldn't fight at all. They were called **conscientious objectors** or 'conshies'.

! WISE UP WORDS

patriotism   recruitment   propaganda
conscription   conscientious objectors

WORK

1 Write a sentence or two to explain the following words:
   patriotism • recruitment • propaganda
   • conscientious objector • conscription

2 a Make a list of all the reasons why you think young men joined up to fight.

   b Do you think young people today are as patriotic as those in 1914? Explain your answer, giving reasons for your opinions.

   c Groups of friends who joined up together were kept together in 'Pals Battalions'. What were the advantages and disadvantages of this?

3 Study all the recruitment posters carefully.

   a For each one, write a sentence explaining:
   • who the poster was appealing to;
   • how it was trying to appeal to them;
   • how successful you think it might have been.

   b Why not design your own Great War recruitment poster? Use the posters on these pages for inspiration.

Trench warfare

AIMS

▸ Where did the fighting take place?
▸ Why did each side build trenches?

Despite what many people thought, the Great War was not 'over by Christmas' in 1914. Far from it, the war was to drag on for four years and three months.

So why did the war last so long? What was it like for the men who fought in it? Why did their views about joining up change as the years passed by?

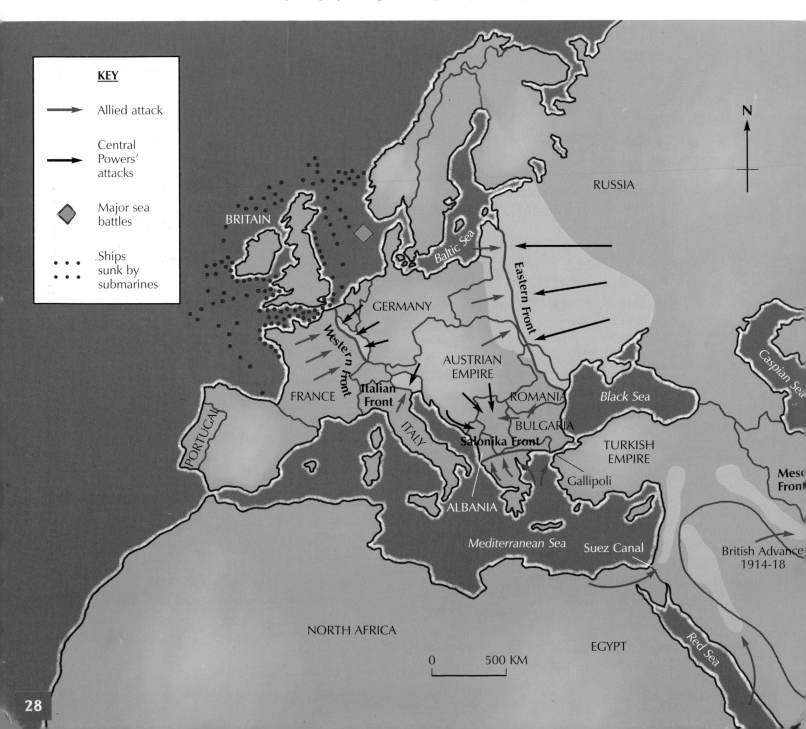

KEY

→ Allied attack

→ Central Powers' attacks

◆ Major sea battles

⋮ Ships sunk by submarines

The Great War was fought mainly in Europe. The areas where the armies fought against each other were called 'fronts'. The biggest was the **Western Front** (in Belgium and France) where French, British and Belgium soldiers tried to stop the Germans advancing to the Channel coast. As enemy soldiers faced each other, they dug deep trenches to protect themselves. Soon, long lines of trenches stretched for over 400 miles between the English Channel and Switzerland.

There was an **Eastern Front** too where Russians fought against Germans and Austrians. There was also fighting in Turkey (who joined in on Germany's side) and Italy (who joined in on Britain's side) as well as at sea and in the air. When war broke out in 1914, most of the people of Europe were pleased. Millions joined up to fight straight away. War seemed exciting, a chance for glory perhaps. However, it didn't take long for these dreams to disappear as 'trench warfare', as the actual fighting was known, turned into a bloody slaughter.

Most of the fighting was done by foot soldiers (infantry), who spent their days in the trenches they had built in the earth to protect themselves. Those trenches were protected with sandbags and barbed wire. They were defended by men with rifles, **bayonets**, machine-guns and **hand grenades**. A few hundred metres away, the enemy did the same. In between was an area called **no man's land**, a dead world full of bomb craters and rotting human remains.

Occasionally, the soldiers would try to capture each other's trenches. The attackers would run across no man's land towards the enemy trenches – the defenders would try to pick them off with rifle fire and machine-guns. For the loss of 50 000 men (yes, 50 000 human beings!), one side might move forward for a week or two and gain a few hundred metres of muddy, useless ground. A week later, for the loss of even more men, they might be pushed back into their original trenches. Unbelievably, despite the loss of millions of men, the Western Front didn't move more than a few miles either way in over four years of war! This was **stalemate** – a complete inability to move forward and a solid determination not to be pushed back. In 1915, Earl Kitchener summed up the stalemate when he said, 'I don't know what is to be done ... but this isn't war'!

▼ **Source B** A description of trench warfare, taken from the 1979 film *All Quiet on the Western Front*. The film is based on a book by Erich Maria Remarque.

'For months now we have fought over a hundred yards of earth. They attack our trench, we attack their trench, then to keep the score even, they will attack our trench once again.'

◄ **Source A** Where the Great War was fought, 1914–1918

! WISE UP WORDS

Western Front   Eastern Front   bayonets
hand grenades   no man's land   stalemate

▶ **Source C** A German soldier's description of a British attack. 'Over the top' was the expression used when soldiers left their trenches and ran towards the enemy.

'At noon we went over the top. After less than 100 yards we came up against an almost concrete wall of whistling and whining machine-gun bullets. The company commander had his face shot away; another man yelling and whimpering held his hands to his belly and, through his fingers, his stomach protruded [stuck out]. A young boy cried for his mother, bright red blood pouring out from his face.'

▼ **Source D** A painting called *Repelling a German Counter-attack* by Frank Dadd. German soldiers run across no man's land to try to capture the British trenches. Look for: i) the different weapons used to stop the enemy; ii) the soldiers who are not joining in with the defence – why do you think they have stopped fighting?

WORK

1 Work out which of the following sentences are true and which are false. Copy out <u>all</u> the sentences, correcting each false one as you write.

  a A 'front' is an area where fighting takes place.

  b All the fighting took place in Europe.

  c The largest front was the Eastern Front.

  d The Western Front stretched for 200 miles through France and Belgium from the English Channel to <u>Swaziland.</u>

  e Stalemate is the word used to describe the situation for many soldiers during the Great War – neither side could move forwards and neither side wanted to retreat.

2 Look at **Source D**.

  a Write a paragraph to describe this painting. You are not allowed to answer in less than 20 words, but do not use more than 100 words.

  b Use this painting and your own knowledge to explain why trench warfare made it difficult for either side to advance.

3 Look at **Source E**.

  a Choose five words to describe no man's land.

  b How do you think this area got its name?

▲ **Source E** An area of no man's land, recently captured by British soldiers. Look for: i) the dead trees, stripped of all their branches by bomb explosions; ii) the bomb craters full of water after heavy rainfall.

Trench life

▶ What was it like in a front-line trench?
▶ What everyday difficulties did the soldiers face?

Month after month, year after year, soldiers battled out the war in what must have been the toughest conditions they had ever seen. Basically, they were 'living rough' and had to cope with all the problems associated with the cold, the wet and the mud.

The soldier – he'd spend about one week in a front-line trench facing the enemy, four weeks in a support trench (about 100 metres behind the front line) and eight weeks in a reserve trench (about 300 metres behind the support trench).

Machine-gun – the most common German gun was the G8, whilst the British favoured the *Vickers*, the *Hotchkiss* or the Lewis Gun.

Sandbags – to protect soldiers from bullets and bombs.

Latrine (toilet) – a board with a hole in it, laid over a pit. Soldiers didn't really like using the latrines – the enemy usually knew where they were located and fired bombs at them in case anyone was using them at the time!

Dugout – for resting and sheltering. The officers (men in charge of the ordinary foot soldiers) often had a bed and table in here.

Periscope – useful for peering over the top of the parapet to spy on the enemy.

Firestep – the raised step where soldiers stood to fire over the parapet (top of the trench).

<u>Daily work</u> – soldiers didn't fight all the time. About one third of the men were on guard duty at any one time, whilst another third collected food, water, letters, ammunition, first aid and so on. The other third repaired the trenches like this soldier.

<u>Health</u> – the trenches could be red hot in the summer and a freezing mass of mud in the winter. Not surprisingly, many suffered from ill health – ulcers, boils, rashes, pneumonia, tuberculosis, dysentery and bronchitis! Spending days on end knee-deep in water could lead to **trench foot**, a painful condition where the foot swells up and develops open sores.

FACT: ▶ Back to 'Blighty'

▶ The effects of trench foot were terrible. The feet would rot and often have to be amputated. Believe it or not, some soldiers *deliberately* tried to get trench foot and other injuries in order to be sent back to Britain. This was known as 'catching a Blighty one' – a wound that doesn't kill, but is serious enough to get you sent back to 'Blighty' – a nickname for Britain.

<u>Hygiene</u> – keeping clean was almost impossible, so almost all soldiers were infested with **lice**, small insects which feed off blood. Their bites caused severe itching and could lead to much more serious illnesses. Rats were a major problem too. A pair of them can produce 880 babies in a year!

<u>Food</u> – food was basic – tinned beef or maconochie (stew) eaten with bread or hard biscuits – but for some of the poorer soldiers, it was the best they'd ever had. Bacon, cheese and jam were treats and the water tasted of chlorine (like in the swimming baths), which killed any germs. Nonetheless, for most soldiers, the food came regularly and was edible!

<u>**Duckboards**</u> – to cover the slippery, muddy trench floor.

33

Source A A front-line trench, 1916. The section of trench was held by Australian troops, fighting as part of the British Empire. Look for: i) the duckboards over the mud at the bottom of the trench; ii) the firestep; iii) the hand-held machine-gun; iv) the periscope being used to spy on the Germans.

▾ **Source D** Written by a German soldier, Otto Dix. The liquor he refers to is the cup of alcohol (usually rum) given to the troops before they went 'over the top'.

'Lice, rats, barbed wire, fleas, shells, bombs, underground caves, corpses, blood, liquor, mice, cats, artillery, filth, bullets, mortars, fire, steel: that is what war is. It is the work of the devil.'

▾ **Source B** A British soldier's experience of a rat-infected trench

'There are millions! Some are huge fellows, nearly as big as cats. Several of our men were awakened to find a rat snuggling down under the blanket alongside them.'

FACT: ▶ 'Stop chatting at the back!'

▶ The soldiers' nickname for a louse was a 'chat'. To get rid of any lice, the soldiers used to sit around together and pop their lice with their thumbnails or burn them off with the flame of a candle. They used to talk to each other as they did it. The soldiers used to call this 'chatting'. Even today, we still use the word 'chatting' to describe a group of people sitting together and talking.

▾ **Source C** Adapted from 'A Victorian Son: An Autobiography 1897–1922' by Stuart Cloete (1973)

'Our trench was dug where a battle had taken place the year before. The ground was full of dead soldiers; they became part of the trench walls. I once fell and put my hand straight through the belly of a long-dead Frenchman. It felt like soft cheese and I remember wondering if I could die from infection. It was days before I got the smell out of my fingernails!'

! WISE UP WORDS

trench foot   lice   duckboards   parapet
firestep   periscope   censor

WORK

1 What was i) trench foot ii) 'a Blighty one' iii) 'chatting'?

2 a Imagine you are a war reporter. Write out a list of ten questions you would have asked a soldier in the trenches. At least four of your questions __must__ cover:
   • daily work
   • health
   • food
   • living conditions
   b Now write the answers a soldier may have given you.
   c Before any report could appear in a British newspaper, a Government official would **censor** (cut out or erase) any information that might damage morale back home or lead to less people supporting the war or joining up to fight. With a pencil or red pen, underline any information in the report that you think the censor would not allow.
   d In what ways has 'censorship', as this was known, changed your report?

The world's deadliest weapons, 1914

AIMS
▶ What were the most common weapons of the Great War?
▶ How effective were the new weapons?

The Great War was the first war where modern machinery was used on a massive scale. Sadly, it was mainly used to find new ways of killing people. The war saw the introduction of some of the most deadly weapons that the world had ever seen – your task is to judge which you think was most deadly and why.

▼ **Source A** Soldiers awaiting orders with their rifles ready. Note that they have swapped their bayonets for barbed wire cutters fitted to the ends of their rifles.

Weapon No. 2

Machine-gun

Although invented in 1862, the machine-gun was still an untested weapon of war. However, it soon became recognised as one of the war's deadliest weapons. A water-cooled machine-gun like the *Vicker* gun could fire up to ten bullets *per second*. In the first 12 days of fighting, the French reported losses of over 200 000 men, mostly through machine-gun fire. According to British estimates, machine-guns caused about 40% of all wounds inflicted on British troops during the war.

▼ **Source B** British machine-gunners in 1916. These guns made it easy to defend a position provided the operators had good cover. Look for: i) the ammunition belt being fed, right to left, by the second member of the gun crew; ii) the basic gas masks.

Weapon No. 1

The Rifle

Each man who joined the British Army was issued with a Lee-Enfield bolt-action rifle and a 40 centimetre steel bayonet to fit onto the end. These rifles were slow (approximately 20 bullets fired per minute) compared to machine-guns, but very accurate. **Snipers** used them very effectively to 'pick off' any soldier who lifted his head above his parapet.

Weapon No. 3

Artillery

Artillery is another word for the large, heavy guns that could shoot bombs (or **shells** as they were known) over long distances. It was common to bombard the enemy trenches for several hours before starting an attack in the hope you might kill lots of soldiers as they sheltered in their dugouts. In 1915, 400 000 shells (some as big as soldiers) were fired every month on the Western Front. Some big guns could fire shells over a distance of 13 miles. When they exploded, the red-hot metal splinters (called shrapnel) would cut an enemy to pieces. The noise damaged men's brains and made their ears bleed. It caused **shell-shock**, a condition similar to a 'nervous breakdown'. Artillery was responsible for about 60% of all wounds.

Weapon No. 4

Gas

The first ever gas attack was on 22 April 1915. The Germans released gas from cylinders and allowed the wind to carry it over French soldiers on the front line. The French panicked and ran. A six-kilometre gap opened up in the French lines but the Germans didn't have enough men to mount a serious assault (although they did take 2 000 prisoners!). An opportunity like this never happened again but gas proved its worth as a weapon of terror. Soon both sides were using gas. There were two types:

Chlorine gas (or phosgene) – this suffocated the lungs and left the victim gasping for air.

Mustard gas – rotted the body – skin blistered, eyes bulged. A victim would cough up the lining of his lungs in clots. The pain was so intense that victims often had to be tied down!

▼ **Source C** *Gassed* by John Singer Sargent. An early gas mask consisted of a handkerchief, dipped in urine and tied over the face! In total, gas caused 15% of all casualties (wounded and killed) in the war. By 1918, one artillery shell in four was a gas shell but, by then, effective gas masks had been developed.

Weapon No. 5

Tanks

Tanks were first used in battle in 1916. This British invention scared the Germans so much that they panicked and fled. However, these armour-plated machines could only travel at about four miles per hour (the fastest, the *Whippet*, had a top speed of eight miles per hour!) and broke down easily. Despite this, the British and French produced over 5 000 whilst the Germans made only 20.

At the Battle of Cambrai in 1917, over 400 British tanks crossed no man's land, broke through barbed wire and crushed machine-gun nests to clear the way for foot soldiers behind them.

Weapon No. 6

The flame-thrower

A canister of oil was strapped to a soldier's back and forced through a nozzle to 'fire' at enemy soldiers. The oil was ignited by a spark to create a sheet of flame that could travel up to 15 metres. Hand-held **flame-throwers** were deadly in small spaces, like dugouts, and caused panic if one was spotted during an attack. Defending soldiers would try and shoot the canister of oil before it got anywhere near. One British soldier who saw a German flame-thrower in action said that men who were caught in the blast of the flame 'were never seen again'!

▼ **Source D** Some towns collected money to buy their own tank to donate to the troops on the front lines. This is an artist's impression of a tank that was paid for by the people of Dudley, West Midlands. It went on a tour of the town before being sent to France.

▲ **Source E** A flame thrower in action

! **WISE UP WORDS**

snipers   artillery   shells   shell-shock
chlorine gas   mustard gas   flame-thrower

WORK

1 a Draw this puzzle into your book and fill in the
answers to the clues.

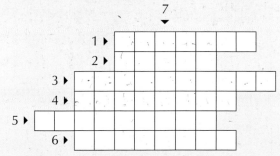

1 This type of gas burns the skin.
2 First used in battle in 1916.
3 Can fire up to ten bullets a second.
4 Razor-sharp splinters of metal.
5 Caused nearly 60% of all wounds.
6 Also known as phosgene gas.

b Now read *down* the puzzle (clue 7). Write a
sentence or two about this word.

2 a Copy out and complete this chart in your book.

WEAPON: List the six major weapons here.	RANGE: Is it a short (0-100 metres), medium (100–1 mile) or long (1 mile+) range weapon?	KILLING POWER: Has it low (1 death at a time), medium (2–10 deaths) or high (10+) killing power?	Is it a weapon used mainly for attack, defence or both?

b In your opinion, which was the Great War's most
deadly weapon? Back up your opinion with facts
and figures.

c In general, do the weapons used in the Great War
make it easier for an army to attack or defend?

Were the 'lions' *really* 'led by donkeys'?

▸ How effective were some of the decisions made by army generals during the Great War?

▸ Why does the Battle of the Somme, 1916, appear in *The Guinness Book of World Records*?

A German army commander once described the British army as 'lions led by donkeys'. He admired the great bravery of the ordinary British soldiers who went into battle, but felt that the generals who were in charge of them were fools. Field Marshall Sir Douglas Haig, who was in charge of the British army from 1915 to 1918, has even been called a 'butcher' for allowing so many men to die. But is this criticism of Haig and his generals fair? Were they 'donkeys' or just men who were trying their best to win a very difficult war?

▾ **Source A** Haig wrote this just before the Battle of the Somme, 1916. Haig believed in a 'war of attrition'. **Attrition** is another word for 'wearing down'.

'The nation must be taught to bear losses. No amount of skill on the part of the commanders, no training, however good, no superiority of arms and ammunition, however great, will enable victories to be won without the sacrifice of men... The nation must be prepared to see heavy casualty lists ... three years of war and the loss of one-tenth of Britain's men is not too great a price to pay.'

▾ **Source B** Before the Battle of the Somme, the generals assured their troops that the shells would destroy the enemy before the men went into battle.

'You will be able to go over the top with a walking stick, you will not need rifles ... you will find the Germans all dead, not even a rat will have survived.'

▾ **Source C** From Brooman's 'The Great War', 1991. The number of dead soldiers appears in *The Guinness Book of Records* as the 'greatest number of casualties in one battle'!

'On that first day of the Battle of the Somme, 20 000 British soldiers were killed and 35 000 wounded, but this did not make General Haig want to change his methods. He ordered more attacks but the same tragic story was repeated each time. Against the advice of experts who said he did not have enough, he sent fifty tanks into the battle in September. Twenty-nine broke down before they even reached the battlefield and the rest soon got stuck in the mud. By the end of the battle, the British and French had lost 620 000 men and the Germans 450 000. The allies had advanced 15 kilometres at the furthest point.'

Source D From a modern history textbook

'One regiment, the first Newfoundlanders, left the trenches with 752 men on the first day of the Battle of the Somme. 684 (or 91%) were killed or wounded in half an hour. No Germans were killed.'

Source E Dead German soldiers at the Battle of the Somme, 1916. The British fired over a million shells at the German trenches for five days. Most escaped harm by digging very deep dugouts (German spy planes had seen men getting ready to attack) but this dugout suffered a direct hit.

▼ **Source F** Haig believed that wearing the enemy down was the key to success. He said this after two weeks of the battle.

'In another six weeks the enemy will find it hard to get enough men.'

▼ **Source G** This quote is taken from the autobiography of the German general Ludendorff, 'My War Memories, 1914–1918', written in 1919.

'We had heavy losses in men and material. As a result of the Somme we were completely exhausted on the Western Front.'

▼ **Source H** One of Haig's generals said this in 1915 when told that the Battle of Loos had cost 60 000 lives.

'What the hell does that matter? There are plenty more men in Britain.'

▼ **Source I** From official German army records of the 27th Infantry Division.

'In the Somme fighting of 1916, we lost our best men. The men who joined after had not the temper, the hardness or the spirit of the men who had fallen.'

▼ **Source J** One of Haig's generals said this about the area where the Battle of Passchendaele (1917) was fought. In it, Britain lost 400 000 men – many had drowned in a sea of stinking, liquid mud. As the dead bodies rotted, the generals in their headquarters could smell decaying flesh from six miles away!'

'My God, did we really send men to fight in that?'

Source K An artist's impression of the statue of Field Marshall Haig in London. Recently, there has been a campaign to get it removed. Some say that the memorial should be a statue of an ordinary soldier, not of the general who sent so many to their deaths. What do you think?

Source L Even when writing in 1926, Haig believed that the horse was going to be very important for the future of warfare. He was often criticised for not accepting new ideas. During the Great War, he felt that machine-guns were hardly needed. The Prime Minister had to order him to send more to the front lines.

'The horse is the future. Aeroplanes and tanks only aid the man and his horse and I feel sure that as time goes on you will find just as much use for the horse – the well-bred horse – as you have ever done in the past.'

! WISE UP WORD

attrition

HUNGRY FOR MORE? Design your own national war memorial to the soldiers who died in the Great War.

WORK

1 Look at **Source A**. What impression does this source give of Field Marshall Haig? You might like to write down two or three sentences to describe him. Start your first sentence, 'Source A makes me think that Haig was…'

2 Look at **Source C**. Does your impression of Haig change after reading this source? Give reasons for your answer.

3 a Write down at least three facts about the Battle of the Somme.
   b Why does the Battle of the Somme feature in *The Guinness Book of Records*?

4 a What is meant by a 'war of attrition'?
   b What evidence is there on these pages that Haig was a firm believer in this type of warfare?

5 Look at **Sources C**, **G** and **I**. Is there any evidence in these sources that Haig's plan to win the Battle of the Somme was successful?

6 a Do the ordinary soldiers who fought in the Great War deserve to be pitied or admired? Explain your answer carefully.
   b In your opinion, was Haig a 'butcher' for allowing thousands of men to needlessly die or was he just trying to do his job and win the war?

Shot at Dawn: the story of Private Harry Farr

▶ What was 'shell-shock'?
▶ Was Harry Farr a coward or a defenceless victim?

Some soldiers found the horrors of war too much to cope with. They suffered from shell-shock brought on by their experiences. Today, we would call it PTSD (Post Traumatic Stress Disorder). Some men shook violently, unable to speak; others became paralysed, suffered panic attacks or cried constantly. The British soldier in **Source A** suffered from shell-shock and it made his life a living hell. He responded to nothing other than the word 'bomb'. He lay perfectly still for hours on end until he heard the word – then he immediately tried to hide!

Shell-shock *was* recognised as an illness in 1915 and could be treated through rest, hypnosis, counselling and even electric shock therapy. After treatment, men would be sent back to their trenches, but sometimes it wasn't treated at all. Some officers felt that certain shell-shock victims were being 'cowardly' and using it as an excuse to get out of the war. Many ordinary soldiers, broken by months of constant shelling and fear of death, simply ran away because they couldn't stand the noise any longer. When found, some of these men were charged with offences like **desertion** or **cowardice**. If found guilty, they would be shot. In total, the British shot 306 men for desertion or cowardice. The French shot 600. In contrast, the Americans and Australians shot none of their own soldiers.

Your task on these four pages is to consider the case of Private Harry Farr, an ordinary soldier from the West Yorkshire Regiment (see **Source B**). He was put on trial (**court martial**) on 2 October 1916 charged with 'cowardice'. He was found guilty and, as military law directed at the time, was shot dead at 6:00am on 18 October 1916.

But was the verdict correct? Was Private Farr *really* a coward? Or was he suffering from shell-shock? Should he have been in hospital rather than in front of a firing squad?

Background

Private Harry Farr, who lived in London with his wife and baby daughter, had been in the army since 1908. He had been fighting in France for nearly two years. On three occasions, between 1915 and 1916, he had reported sick with his nerves. He had been in hospital three times, once for a stay of five months. During that stay, he shook so much that a nurse had to write his letters home to his wife. During September, he reported sick again. But, as he wasn't physically wounded, he was told to get back to the front-line trenches. These adapted notes from his court martial tell what happened next.

◄ **Source A** A shell-shock victim

Court Martial at Ville-Sur-Ancre, 2 October 1916

Alleged Offender: No. 8871 Private Harry T FARR 1st Battalion – West Yorkshire Regiment.

Offence Charged: Section 4. (7) Army Act: Misbehaving before the enemy in such a manner as to show cowardice.

Plea: Not Guilty.

◀ **Source B** Private Harry Farr

THE PROSECUTION

1st Witness: Sergeant Major H HAKING

'On 17 September, at about 9:00am, FARR reported to me well behind the lines. He said he was sick but had left his position without permission. He said he couldn't find his commanding officer. I told him to go to the dressing station [a trench hospital]. They sent him back saying he wasn't wounded. I sent him back to the front lines.

At about 8:00pm, his commanding officer (Captain BOOTH) told me FARR was missing again. Later on I saw FARR back where I'd first seen him well behind the line. I asked him why he was there. He said, "I cannot stand it". I asked him what he meant and he repeated, "I cannot stand it". I told him to get back to the front line and he said, "I cannot go". I then told BOOTH and two other men to take him back by force. After going 500 metres, FARR began to scream and struggle. I told him that if he didn't go back he would be on trial for cowardice. He said, "I'm not fit to go to the trenches". I then said I'd take him to a doctor but he refused to go saying, "I will not go any further". I ordered the men to carry on but FARR again started struggling and screaming. I told the men to leave him alone and FARR jumped up and ran back to where I'd first seen him early in the day. He was then arrested.'

2nd Witness: Captain J W BOOTH

'On 17 September 1916 at 3:00pm I told FARR to get back up to his trench. Later that evening, I could see he was missing without having received permission. At about 9:00pm, I saw him well away from where he should have been. Sergeant Major HAKING ordered me to take him back to his trench under escort. After about 500 metres, FARR became violent and threatened the three of us. FARR was later arrested.'

3rd Witness: Private D FARREL (one of the soldiers ordered to take FARR back to his trench)

'On 17 September 1916, at about 11:30pm, I was ordered by Captain BOOTH to take FARR back to the trenches. After going 500 metres, he started struggling and saying he wanted to see a doctor. The Sergeant Major said he could see one later. FARR refused to go any further. I tried to pull him along. The Sergeant Major told me to let go and FARR ran off.'

4th Witness: Corporal W FORM

Corporate FORM said exactly the same as Private FARREL, the third witness.

WORK

1 a Write a sentence or two to explain these terms:

shell-shock • desertion • cowardice • court martial

   b How many people did the British shoot for cowardice and desertion during the Great War?

2 Up to this point, what is your impression of i) Sergeant Major Haking and ii) Private Harry Farr?

THE DEFENCE

Harry Farr was not given an opportunity to ask someone to help him with his defence. Instead, he defended himself.

1st Witness: The accused, Private H FARR

'On 16 September 1916, I started to feel sick. I tried to get permission to leave the trenches but couldn't because people were asleep or unavailable. Eventually, I found Sergeant Major HAKING on 17 September at 9:00am and he told me to go to the dressing station. They said I wasn't physically wounded and sent me back to my trench. I started to go but felt sick again so I told an ordinary officer where I was going and went back well behind the front line again.'

'When I saw Sergeant Major HAKING, I told him I was sick again and couldn't stand it. He said, "You're a f****** coward and you'll go back to your trench. I give f*** all for my life and I'd give f*** all for yours so I'll get you f****** well shot". I was then escorted back to my trench. On the way, we met up with another group of soldiers and one asked where I'd been. Sergeant Major HAKING replied, "Ran away, same as he did last night". I said to HAKING that he'd got it in for me.'

'I was then taken towards my trench but the men were shoving me. I told them I was sick enough already. Then Sergeant Major HAKING grabbed my rifle and said, "I'll blow your f****** brains out if you don't go". I called out for help but there was none. I was then tripped up so I started to struggle. Soon after, I was arrested. If no one had shoved me I'd have gone back to the trenches.'

Court Question: Why haven't you been sick since you were arrested?

Answer by FARR: Because I feel much better when I'm away from the shell fire.

2nd Witness: Sergeant J ANDREWS

'FARR has been sick with his nerves several times.'

Character Witness: Lieutenant L P MARSHALL

'I have known FARR for six weeks. Three times he has asked for leave because he couldn't stand the noise of the guns. He was trembling and didn't appear in a fit state.'

Character Witness: Captain A WILSON

'I cannot say what has destroyed this man's nerves, but on many occasions he has been unable to keep his nerves in action. He causes others to panic. Apart from his behaviour when fighting, his conduct and character are very good.'

The entire court martial took about 20 minutes. Soon after, the judging panel gave its verdict ... GUILTY. They said 'the charge of cowardice is clearly proved and the opinion of Sergeant Major HAKING is that FARR is bad. Even soldiers who know him say that FARR is no good'.

On 14 October 1916, Harry Farr's death sentence was confirmed by Sir Douglas Haig, the man in charge of the British army. He was shot at dawn on 18 October 1916.

He refused to be blindfolded. According to his death certificate, 'death was instantaneous'. He has no known grave and doesn't appear on any war memorials. At first, his widow was told he had been killed in action, but was later told the truth when her war pension was stopped. Widows were not entitled to a pension if their husband had been shot for cowardice.

PAUSE FOR THOUGHT

Try to think about the case of Harry Farr from the army's point of view. Why do you think Sir Douglas Haig, the man in charge of the British army, felt that it was important to execute 'deserters' and 'cowards'?

FACT: ▶ Shell-shock

▶ In 1922, the British War Office Committee announced that shell-shock did not exist and that it was a collection of already known illnesses.

▼ **Source C** The Shot at Dawn memorial is based on a young soldier called Herbert Burden. He joined the army in 1914 aged 16. He lied about his age to join; you had to be 18 to join up. Nearly two years later, he was court-martialled for desertion after running away when he saw his friends killed during a battle. He was shot aged 17 years 10 months, still officially too young to be in the army in the first place!

FACT: ▶ The Shot at Dawn Campaign

▶ In recent years, the relatives of some of the men shot for desertion or cowardice have been campaigning for them to receive **pardons**. They believe that many of them were shell-shocked rather than cowards or deserters. In June 2001, a memorial was erected near Lichfield, Staffordshire, to remember the 306 British soldiers executed by their own side during the Great War. It was unveiled by Mrs Gertrude Harris, the 87-year-old daughter of Private Harry Farr! Despite gaining national publicity, the campaign has so far been unsuccessful.

FACT: ▶ Trigger happy!

▶ The French, British and Italians shot well over 1 000 of their own men. They said the executions were good for discipline. Official figures show that the Germans executed 48.

! WISE UP WORDS

desertion   cowardice   court martial   pardon

WORK

1 a Write a definition of the word 'contradict'.

  b In what ways does Harry Farr's version of events on 17 September 1916 contradict Sergeant Major Haking's?

  c In what ways are the two versions similar?

  d Why do you think it is difficult for two versions of the same event to agree with each other all the time?

2 a In your opinion, was Harry Farr a coward or was he suffering from shell-shock? You should include details from some of the witnesses in your answer.

  b Write two letters.
    The first should be from Sergeant Major Haking, one of the commanding officers of Harry Farr. It was common practice for commanding officers to write home to the family of any dead soldiers in their 'care'. Imagine you are Haking and write a letter to Harry's widow informing her of the situation surrounding his death.
    The second letter to Harry's widow should be from one of Harry Farr's friends, perhaps Captain Wilson.

  c In what ways are the letters similar and/or different? Give reasons for your answer.

How did 'Poppy Day' start?

AIMS
▶ How did the war end?
▶ What are the origins of 'Remembrance Day'?

1917 was a vital year in the course of the war. Ordinary Russian people rebelled against their leaders (they murdered their king and his entire family!) and stopped fighting the Germans. Germany now concentrated all of its soldiers, guns, gas, ships and planes on fighting the British and the French. However, by then, the USA had joined the war on the side of Britain and France.

The Germans now tried desperately to defeat the British and French before the fresh American soldiers arrived at the front lines. But, despite an all-out attack, the Germans could not break through. The German soldiers started to **retreat**. Back home in Germany, the **civilians** had reached breaking point – they were starving and there were riots in the streets. Soon, the countries on Germany's side began to surrender – and German troops were exhausted too. Eventually, Germany's King (Kaiser Wilhelm II) ran away to Holland and the government that replaced him called for a **ceasefire**. At 11:00am on 11 November 1918, the Great War was over.

▶ **Source A** The front page of the *Daily Mirror*, 12 November 1918. Some celebrations lasted for three days – the police had to be sent to break them up in the end. It was the same in most of the major cities all over Europe.

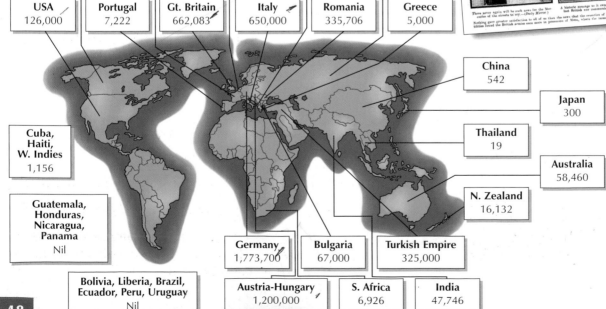

Canada	France	Belgium	Serbia	Russia
56,119	1,375,000	13,716	45,000	1,700,000

USA	Portugal	Gt. Britain	Italy	Romania	Greece
126,000	7,222	662,083	650,000	335,706	5,000

China
542

Japan
300

Thailand
19

Australia
58,460

N. Zealand
16,132

Cuba, Haiti, W. Indies
1,156

Guatemala, Honduras, Nicaragua, Panama
Nil

Germany
1,773,700

Bulgaria
67,000

Turkish Empire
325,000

Bolivia, Liberia, Brazil, Ecuador, Peru, Uruguay
Nil

Austria-Hungary
1,200,000

S. Africa
6,926

India
47,746

◀ **Source B** War deaths 1914–1918. As you can see, it is little wonder that many people began calling it a World War. Soon after the end of the war, an outbreak of influenza (flu) swept across Europe and killed an estimated 25 million more people!

▼ **Source C** Some of the soldiers' bodies were never found, they just sank into the mud where they had died. Even today, French and Belgian farmers still find skeletons of dead soldiers when working on their fields.

The war did terrible damage to the land on which it was fought. In France, where most of the fighting took place, an area the size of Wales was ruined. Buildings, roads, trees and hedgerows just disappeared. Only one living thing seemed to flourish – the poppy. For many soldiers, the poppy had become a symbol of life and hope amongst all the fighting. The poppies continued to grow after the soldiers left the trenches in 1918.

▼ **Source D** A Remembrance Day poppy. We buy our poppy as a token, to make a personal statement that we remember those who fought for their country. A popular poem of 1918 went:

'When you get home
Tell them of us and say
For your tomorrow
We gave our today.'

! WISE UP WORDS

retreat   civilians   ceasefire

In 1919, some of the poppies were collected and sold to raise money for war widows and injured soldiers. Soon artificial ones were being made in a factory in London and sold all over Britain. In the same year, the Government received a letter from Percy Fitzpatrick, whose son had been killed in France in 1917. Percy suggested that two minutes' silence be observed on the anniversary of the end of the war. King George V agreed. Today, the two-minute silence is held on the nearest Sunday after the anniversary of the end of the Great War – it is called Remembrance Sunday and poppies are sold to raise money to help those people affected by all wars. Some people call it 'Poppy Day'.

FACT: ▶ How many?

▶ Every year, over 30 million poppies are sold. The Poppy Appeal raises about £20 million a year.

WORK

1 a Why was 1917 such an important year in the war?

   b When exactly did the war end?

   c How do we remember the end of the Great War today?

2 Look at **Source B**.

   a Turn these figures into either a bar chart or a pie chart.

   b In total, how many people were killed in the Great War?

3 Look at **Source C**. Write a short description of the photograph.

4 Look at **Source D**.

   a Copy out the picture of the poppy and write the poem next to your picture.

   b Write a paragraph explaining what the poem means.

   c Why was the poppy used as a symbol of the Great War?

   d Have you ever bought a poppy? If not, say why not. If so, explain why you bought one – did you know how your money was used?

Have you been learning?

Task 1 The poor in 1900

In 1901, Seebohm Rowntree looked at the lives of poor people in York. In his report, he said that many people lived below the 'poverty line' (the minimum amount of money a person needed to buy proper food, clothing and shelter). Rowntree said that no matter how hard a person worked, there were certain times when they couldn't help falling below the 'poverty line'.

Study the graph below carefully. It appeared in Rowntree's report, *Poverty: A Study of Town Life*, published in 1901.

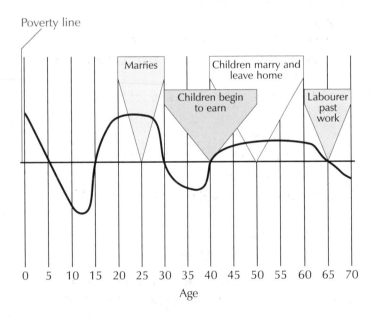

a Draw and label a neat copy of this chart in your book.

b Write down the three times in a lifetime when a person fell below the line. For each time, explain why it happened.

c How were poor people, particularly children, helped in Britain from 1906 onwards? You may need to look again at pages 8 and 9 to refresh your memory.

Task 2 A *Titanic* wordsearch

This wordsearch includes 12 words associated with *Titanic*. Search carefully for each word, writing it down every time you find one. Next to each word, write a sentence or fact that demonstrates your understanding of the topic.

As an example, one has been done for you.

R	M	A	V	B	E	L	F	A	S	T	T	N	O	K
I	W	I	M	I	O	A	I	M	A	I	D	E	N	F
G	N	I	C	S	I	C	B	F	O	G	C	C	E	W
K	A	O	L	E	I	S	T	E	E	R	A	G	E	B
O	S	G	T	G	B	C	M	H	G	B	A	C	E	T
E	X	B	R	P	N	E	I	A	Y	E	O	E	S	E
L	P	H	T	I	M	S	R	T	Y	G	S	A	S	L
K	J	R	R	I	D	A	E	G	N	T	E	R	T	F
A	U	E	M	G	F	B	H	R	C	A	A	A	B	S
N	W	S	S	T	E	P	H	T	N	S	L	A	R	R
A	R	T	S	E	H	C	R	O	U	T	E	T	G	D
X	G	Y	M	N	A	S	I	U	M	O	N	E	A	I
I	B	A	I	H	T	A	P	R	A	C	S	U	T	Y

ISMAY: Bruce Ismay was in charge of the White Star Line, the owners of *Titanic*. He escaped on Collapsible Lifeboat C at 1:40am.

Task 3 Murder in Sarajevo, 28 June 1914

Look at the following eight statements about the events in Sarajevo on 28 June 1914. You may notice that the order of events is all mixed up *and* each statement contains two spelling mistakes.

- The Archduke is unhurt and his car speeds of to his meeting with the mayor at the town haul. He is furious.

- Franz Ferdinand and his wive arrive at Sarajevo raleway station at 9:28am.

- Immediately, Austria-Hungary blames Serba four killing the Archduke and plans an attack.

- The driver takes a rong turn and has to reverse back. At this moment, a Serbian terorist called Gavrilo Princip shoots and kills the Archduke and his wife.

- On there way to the town hall, a bomb is throne at the Archduke's car and the explosion injures several people.

- Princip is arrested and beeten up in jail.

- The Archduck and his wife get into a dark-grean, open-topped car.

- After his meating, the Archduke desides to visit the injured people in hospital.

a With a partner, work out the correct chronological order of events.
b In your book, copy out each statement (in the correct chronological order) *and* correct each spelling mistake as you write.
c The events of 28 June 1914 started a chain reaction that drew most of Europe into a terrible war. Design a flow diagram that charts how each country was dragged into war in the few weeks after 28 June.

Task 4 Odd one out

Here are six groups of words or phrases. In each group there is an odd one out. What do the three words have in common that the fourth does not have? When you think you have found it, write a sentence or two about why you think it doesn't fit in with the others.

a France • Germany • Russia • Great Britain
b parapet • sandbag • duckboard • France
c Great Britain • Germany • Austria-Hungary • Turkey
d volunteer • conscription • recruitment • conscientious objector
e shell • hand-grenade • bayonet • bullet
f mud • tank • machine-gun • rifle

Task 5 Great War anagrams

In the anagram list you will find:

- a new invention in 1916
- something that burns the skin
- another name for foot soldiers
- a specialist soldier who shoots at his enemy one at a time
- a small hand-held bomb
- big guns
- a device used to look over the parapet
- the name of the muddy wasteland between two lines of trenches
- something that can fire hundreds of bullets per minute
- an itchy problem
- the blade attached to the end of a rifle
- missiles fired by big guns
- the planks of wood used to cover up a muddy trench floor
- a painful disease
- a small trench-loving rodent

All the answers are given below, but the words and letters have been mixed up. Can you unravel them?

ENTCHR TFOO • PEIRSN • NHDA ARNDEEG

• LRATYRILE • ON AMN'S ADNL • OBDDCKSARU

• ISORPECEP • RTA • KTASN • TMDSAUR AGS

• AIMCHNE-NUG • CELI • YNBTOAE • LHLSES

• IYAFNRNT

How did women win the vote?

AIMS
▸ Who were the suffragettes?
▸ How did the Great War affect the roles of women?

Look at **Source A** carefully. This poster appeared in 1900 and demonstrates how many men felt about the idea of giving women the right to vote. What is the poster trying to say about a woman's mind?

▾ **Source A** 'A woman's mind magnified'

A WOMAN'S MIND
MAGNIFIED

In 1900, no woman in Britain had the right to vote. Men ruled the nation from Parliament and women were expected to keep out of the way. It was widely believed (by men of course) that a woman's place was in the home, looking after their children and husband. If any woman had a job, it would always be lower paid than a man's ... and women were restricted to jobs as teachers, nannies, cleaners, nurses and factory workers.

Some women no longer accepted this and one group started a campaign to get women the vote. They thought that if women could vote, they might be able to elect MPs that promised to improve their lives (get women equal pay with men for example). This group held meetings, wrote letters to Parliament and went on marches. They weren't very successful!

Another group decided that the only way to get the country's attention was to get violent and become a nuisance. If they annoyed enough people, then Parliament might give in and grant women the vote. This group were known as the **suffragettes** – **suffrage** is another word for 'vote'.

▸ **Source B** The suffragettes did all they could to get public attention. They smashed shop windows, threw eggs at politicians and even chained themselves to the railings outside Buckingham Palace.

▸ **Source C** After 1912, the suffragette campaign grew more violent. They set fire to churches, railway stations and post boxes. They poured acid on golf course putting greens and even tipped purple dye into a reservoir outside Bradford. Many women were arrested but went on hunger strike. The Government reacted by ordering all **hunger strikers** to be force-fed by pouring soup through a tube up their nose or down their throat!

In 1914, the Great War started and the suffragettes stopped their campaign of violence. Instead, they put their full support behind helping Britain to win the war. But the war brought women an unexpected opportunity. With more and more men leaving their jobs to become soldiers, women got the chance to do jobs they had never done before. They became bus drivers, milk deliverers, police officers, railway ticket collectors and car mechanics. Thousands worked in **munitions** factories (which were very unhealthy and dangerous), or became nurses or ambulance drivers near the front lines in France.

▼ **Source D** A photograph of women mending a road during the Great War

▼ **Source E** Prime Minister Herbert Asquith, speaking in August 1916. What do you think he means by women's 'special claim'?

'It is true that women cannot fight with rifles, but they have aided in the most effective way in the war. What is more, when the war comes to an end, don't women have a special claim to be heard on the many questions which affect their interests? I cannot deny that claim.'

! **WISE UP WORDS**

suffragettes   suffrage   hunger strike
munitions

▼ **Source F** A comparison of the quality and output in factories of men and women in 1918. It is little wonder that Herbert Asquith said, 'How could we carry on the war without women? There is hardly a service in which women have not been at least as active as men.'

Quality:
Metal – women's work better than men's
Aircraft woodwork – women equal to men
Bullet making – women equal to men
Shell making – women's work poorer than men's

Quantity:
Metal – women's production equal to men's
Aircraft woodwork – women's production equal to men's
Bullet making – women's production equal to men's; in some cases, women produce 20% more than men
Shell making – women's production behind men

By the end of the war, many people felt that women had earned the right to vote – and many MPs didn't want the suffragettes to start their violent campaign again! In 1918, Parliament changed the voting laws and gave all men over 21 and all women over 30 the right to vote (as long as they owned their own house or were married to a man who did). Ten years later, Parliament reduced the voting age for women to 21, regardless of whether they owned a house or were married or not. Finally, women had the same political rights as men.

WORK

1 Look at **Source A**.
   a Explain what is meant by the word 'sexist'.
   b In what ways is **Source A** sexist?

2 Look at **Source B**.
   a Who were the 'suffragettes' and what tactics did they use to try to win the vote?
   b What were the dangers of these tactics?
   c What else could the suffragettes have done to get publicity?

3 In what way did the Great War give many women an unexpected opportunity?

4 a When did all women finally achieve the same political status as men?
   b In your opinion, what helped the cause of 'Votes for Women' the most – the suffragettes or the Great War? Give reasons for your answer.

HISTORY MYSTERY

Emily Davison – suicide or protest?

The Derby is one of the most famous horse races in the world. Huge crowds, including many members of the Royal Family, flock to watch it every year at Epsom Racecourse in Surrey.

In 1913, a suffragette named Emily Davison was killed by the King's horse, Anmer. 20 000 people attended her funeral and the leaders of the suffragettes claimed that Davison had died for the cause of 'Votes for Women'. But had she? Was Davison trying to kill herself – or was this just a tragic accident? Was it suicide – or just a protest that went badly wrong?

Now it's time for you, History Mystery detective, to look through the evidence and come to your conclusion.

EVIDENCE A Emily Davison's prison record. She was a very **militant** suffragette who believed in 'deeds not words'. What do you think this meant?

March 1909 One month in prison for obstruction (blocking a road)

September 1909 Two months for stone throwing

November 1909 One month for stone throwing

November 1910 One month for breaking windows

January 1912 Six months for setting fire to post boxes

November 1912 Ten days for assaulting a vicar who she mistook for a Member of Parliament

EVIDENCE B From a book by G Colmore, 'The Life of Emily Davison', 1913. The Suffragette Summer Festival was a week-long meeting of hundreds of suffragettes.

'She was able to go to the [Suffragette Summer] Festival on the opening day, Tuesday 3 June. Emily was never brighter than on that day. She stayed long at the fair and said she should come every day, "except tomorrow. I'm going to the Derby tomorrow".

"What are you going to do?"

"Ah ha!"

It was her usual answer … when she had planned something. "Look in the evening paper", she added, "and you will see something".'

EVIDENCE C From an eyewitness, John Ervine, who stood near to Emily Davison on the day.

'The King's horse, Anmer, came up and Ms Davison went towards it. She put up her hand, but whether it was to catch hold of the reins or protect herself, I don't know. It was all over in a few seconds. The horse knocked her over with great force and then stumbled and fell, throwing the jockey violently onto the ground. Both he and Ms Davison were bleeding a lot. I feel sure that Ms Davison meant to stop the horse and that she didn't go onto the course thinking the race was over.'

EVIDENCE D From an Internet website, written by a modern historian.

'Some believed that Davison was trying to cross the racecourse and had failed to see that not all the horses had cleared the course. Other spectators claimed that they heard her shout "Votes for Women" before leaping out in front of the King's horse. A crude black and white film was taken that caught the event "live" … and it shows clearly that Davison stopped in front of Anmer (therefore she did not want to simply cross the course) and it appears that she tried to make a grab for the reins of the horse.'

! WISE UP WORDS

militant   martyr

EVIDENCE E The front page of the *Daily Sketch*, published the day after. Look for: i) the fallen horse; ii) Emily Davison; iii) Emily's hat.

DAILY SKETCH.

HISTORY'S MOST WONDERFUL DERBY: FIRST HORSE DISQUALIFIED: A 100 TO 1 CHANCE WINS: SUFFRAGETTE NEARLY KILLED BY THE KING'S COLT.

EVIDENCE F From Sylvia Pankhurst's 'The Suffrage Movement: An Intimate Account of Persons and Ideals', published in 1931.

'Her friend declared that she would not have died without writing a farewell message to her mother. Yet she sewed the [suffragette] flags inside her coat as though to make sure that no mistake could be made as to her motive when her body was examined.'

EVIDENCE G Part of the official report surrounding Davison's death. She had asked for the flags a few days before the race meeting.

FOUND ON THE BODY OF EMILY DAVISON

OFFICIAL POLICE REPORT

2 large suffragette flags (green, white and purple stripes) pinned inside the back of her coat; 1 purse (containing three shillings, eight pence and three farthings); 8 postage stamps; 1 key; 1 helper pass for the Suffragette Summer Festival, Kensington, London; 1 notebook; 1 handkerchief; some envelopes and writing paper; 1 race card; 1 return half of her railway ticket.

EVIDENCE H Adapted from the writings of Emily Davison herself. These events occurred in Holloway Prison, two weeks before her release on a six-month sentence for arson. What do you think she means when she writes that 'one big tragedy would save many others'?

'As soon as I got the chance I threw myself over the prison railings. The idea in my mind was that one big tragedy would save many others; but the netting prevented any injury. Then I threw myself down on an iron staircase, a distance of 10 to 13 metres, but the netting caught me again. I felt I had only one chance left, so I hurled myself head first down the staircase, a distance of three metres. I landed on my head with a mighty thud and was knocked out. When I recovered I was in agony.'

WORK

There are two main theories about Emily Davison's death. Consider them both.

1 She tried to kill herself for the cause of 'Votes for Women', hoping to turn herself into a **martyr** in the process.

2 She wanted to make a protest by stopping the King's horse but it went badly wrong and she died in a tragic accident.

Reread it all again and consider:

- Why she wanted two flags.
- Why she didn't tell anyone what she planned to do.
- Why she chose the King's horse – or did she go to stop Anmer by chance?

Step 1 Make sure you fully understand ALL the evidence.

Step 2 Find any evidence that Davison was trying to kill herself.

Step 3 Find any evidence to show that Davison did *not* plan to kill herself.

Step 4 You must deliver your verdict.

Imagine you are part of a Government inquiry team who has been given the job of investigating the death in order to arrive at a conclusion.

Give a basic outline of Davison's death. You might include details of Davison herself and the events before she was killed.

Does the inquiry think Emily Davison planned to make a protest or did she plan to die as well? Back up any of your conclusions with evidence. Best of luck!

How did countries try to avoid any more wars?

▶ How were the defeated nations treated after the Great War had ended?
▶ What was the **League of Nations**?

The Great War ended at 11:00am on 11 November 1918. Later that day, David Lloyd George (the British Prime Minister) said the following words in Parliament:

'At eleven o'clock this morning, the cruellest and most terrible war that has ever cursed mankind came to an end. I hope we can say that this morning came to an end all wars.'

Lloyd George was right to call it a cruel and terrible war. By 1918, much of Europe was in a mess – land devastated, farms destroyed, railways blown up and mines flooded. Millions had died – and millions more were weak and starving.

So how did nations try to sort out the mess? Would the winning countries punish the losers? And how would any future wars be avoided?

In January 1919, politicians from the winning countries met at the Palace of Versailles, near Paris, to decide what was to happen to the beaten enemy.

▼ **Source B** The main points of the Treaty of Versailles. All the other losing countries lost land, had their armed forces reduced and had to pay for war damage. However, it was only Germany that was blamed for starting the war.

▲ **Source A** The three most important politicians at the Paris Peace Conference – George Clemenceau of France, Woodrow Wilson of the USA and David Lloyd George of Britain. They were nicknamed **The Big Three**. The Germans, who were top of most people's 'hit list', were not allowed to send anyone to put their viewpoint across. Nor were the Austrian-Hungarians, the Turks or the Bulgarians.

Germany must pay for the war in money and goods. The figure was set at £6 600 million. They must sign to agree that they had started the war too.

Germany to have no air force or submarines. Only tiny army and navy. No tanks or submarines allowed. No German soldiers allowed anywhere near France.

Germany to hand over colonies to Britain and France.

League of Nations set up. All countries should join this so they can talk about their problems rather than fight.

Parts of countries cut off to make new countries.

In June 1919, the politicians announced their decision to the world. Germany's punishments, set out in a huge document called the **Treaty** of Versailles, were the first to be published. German politicians, sent over for the day, were told to sign the peace agreement … or face invasion! They signed.

Source C This appeared on the front page of one of Germany's leading newspapers on the day the Treaty was signed – 28 June 1919. The Hall of Mirrors is a huge mirrored room inside the Palace of Versailles.

VENGEANCE, GERMAN NATION!

'Today, in the Hall of Mirrors, the disgraceful Treaty is being signed. Do not forget it. The German people will regain their place amongst the nations to which they are entitled. Then will come **vengeance** for the shame of 1919.'

After the losers were punished, the winners turned their attentions to trying to stop wars forever. They decided to set up a League of Nations, a kind of international club for settling problems peacefully. Its headquarters would be in Geneva, Switzerland. About 40 countries joined up straight away, hoping to solve any disputes by discussion rather than war. If one nation did end up declaring war on another, all the other member nations would stop trading with the invading country until a lack of supplies would bring the fighting to an end.

The League would aim to help in other ways too. Countries would work together to fight diseases, stop drug smuggling, slavery and improve working conditions. However, less than half the countries in the world joined – Germany wasn't allowed and politicians in the USA voted against it – and it didn't have its own army to go in and stop trouble. Yet, for a few years, it seemed to work well (see **Source D**).

Source D How the League of Nations helped

THE WORK OF THE LEAGUE OF NATIONS

- Sorted out a dispute between Finland and Sweden
- Sorted out a dispute between Greece and Bulgaria
- Limited the hours of work for small children
- Banned the use of a poisonous lead in paint
- Worked hard to defeat diseases such as leprosy, malaria, cholera and smallpox
- Freed 200 000 slaves
- Produced an international highway code for road users
- Worked closely with the governments of Germany, Holland, France and Switzerland to defeat drug smuggling
- Helped 400 000 prisoners of war to get back to their homelands

! WISE UP WORDS

vengeance   The Big Three   League of Nations   Treaty

WORK

1 a Who were The Big Three?
  b Why do you think these men made most of the important decisions after the war had finished?
  c What do you think annoyed the Germans most about the Paris Peace Conference?

2 Look at **Source B**.
  a Make a copy of **Source B**.
  b Describe why the Treaty of Versailles caused so much anger among ordinary Germans.
  c Imagine you had fought in the German army during the Great War. You have been asked to speak to your former comrades about the Treaty. Write a short speech. Remember:
   • you are angry
   • you are trying to make others angry
   • you are biased

Top Tip: You might want to include the following words or phrases:
humiliation of Germany • lost land • weak with such a small army • betrayal of your dead comrades • shame • anger • bitterness • make Germany great again • scrap the Treaty • take back lost land • glory • pride • revenge on France and Britain
Try to write your speech as you would actually say it. Remember that you are trying to encourage people to feel angry. Note: Hitler, who fought for the Germans as an ordinary soldier, started making these sorts of speeches in 1919!

3 a How did the League of Nations try to stop wars?
  b What were its two main weaknesses?
  c In its early years, was the League of Nations a success or not? Give examples to go with your answer.

Different ways to run a country

▶ What is the difference between a democracy and a dictatorship?
▶ What are the main features of each?

No two countries are run in the same way. The United States of America is run differently from France, which, in turn, is run differently from Britain. Laws are different (so are punishments, for example, the death penalty); education, health care and political parties vary – even the side of the road upon which a car can be driven can change from one nation to the next. These differences have been in place for many years; they evolve over time leaving a situation where today, we have hundreds of countries run in hundreds of different ways.

Despite these differences, it is possible to put most countries into one of two categories – **democracies** or **dictatorships**.

It was possible to do this in the 1920s and 1930s too. In fact, the disagreements and arguments about how governments should be organised spilled over into war – another one!

In order to clearly understand your studies on the build up to another world war – World War Two – it is important to know the main features of both a democracy and a dictatorship.

Type of Government

DEMOCRACY

Origins Started in Ancient Greece. Developed gradually over hundreds of years, mainly in Europe and America.

Beliefs Ordinary people have a say in how their country is governed. They vote in regular elections in which there are several political parties to choose from. The people are represented by the organisations they elect – for example, Parliament or councils.

Comments The people have a number of 'freedoms' or rights:

- Freedom of speech (the right to say what you think)

- Freedom of information (the right to read, listen to and watch what you want)

- Freedom of belief (the right to worship any religion)

- Freedom in law (the right to a fair trial – if arrested, 'you have a right to remain silent' too!)

- Freedom of association (the right to join or form a political party, join a trade union or any other organisation – even the Boy Scouts!)

Examples from the 1920s and 1930s Britain, France and the USA

Type of Government
DICTATORSHIP

Origins For thousands of years, some men have tried to totally control others. The controllers are usually backed up by large numbers of supporters and lots of weapons.

Beliefs Ordinary people have no say in how their country is run. There are no regular elections because the country is run by one political party or one man – the **dictator** (usually helped by his 'friends' and his army)

Comments People have very few 'freedoms' or rights:

- There is no free speech (if they criticise their leaders, they are likely to be arrested)
- There is no freedom of information (the dictator controls the newspapers, books, magazines, films and so on)
- Not all religions are allowed – if any!
- There is no legal freedom (the police can arrest whom they want, when they want and keep them in jail without trial)
- People can only join groups or associations allowed by the dictatorship

Examples from the 1920s and 1930s Italy, Spain, USSR (Russia) and Nazi Germany

NO ELECTIONS
(this year or any other)
Signed: *The Dictator*

I'd just like to say that the dictator is an absolute...

⚠ WISE UP WORDS
democracy   dictatorship   dictator

WORK

1. a In your own words, explain what a democracy is. You must use <u>no more</u> than 50 words.

   b In your own words, explain what a dictatorship is. Again, use <u>no more</u> than 50 words.

   c Do <u>you</u> live in a democracy or a dictatorship? Explain how you made your decision.

2. Work with a partner. One of you must choose to describe a dictatorship, the other a democracy. Using only ten words each, explain to your partner the political system you have chosen. They must fully understand what a dictatorship or a democracy is by the end of your presentation.

   - Use drawings to help you.
   - Perhaps you could mime some of the features of your system.
   - Which words will you use? Remember, you're only allowed to use ten words to describe your choice of democracy or dictatorship.
   - Set aside an amount of time to prepare!

At the end of the Great War, many people hoped that democracy would spread to most countries of the world. In fact, many countries did introduce a democratic system when the war ended. Sadly though, some countries were in such a mess after the war (and remained that way), that their newly elected politicians didn't seem to have any solutions to their problems. More and more countries listened to people who promised to make their lives better and their nations great again ... at a cost – DICTATORSHIP. Amazingly, over 30 countries became dictatorships between 1919 and 1939. Unfortunately, some of these dictators would bring about another world war.

Two types of dictatorship

AIMS
▸ What are Fascism and Communism?
▸ In which countries did these two political theories develop?

Powerful nations such as the USA, France and Britain were democratic countries in the 1920s and 1930s (they still are!). However, people in some other nations rejected democracy and turned to dictatorship instead. Some countries, such as Italy, had **Fascist** dictatorships, whilst the USSR (previously Russia) had a **Communist** dictatorship.

These four pages aim to examine the ideas behind **Fascism** and **Communism** and show examples of each in action. You should look for similarities between these two types of dictatorship ... and the major differences too.

A COMMUNIST DICTATORSHIP

CASE STUDY 1: THE USSR

Communism is a theory. It is a set of ideas about a particular way to run a country. It was dreamed up by Karl Marx, a German living in London, in the 1840s. He wrote a book about his theory ... and it turned into a best-seller.

Marx wrote that in a Communist country, everyone would be equal (men <u>and</u> women) and everything would be shared. There would be no different classes and no great differences of wealth. There would be no private property and the government would run farms, factories and businesses for the benefit of all people. There wouldn't be any need for money or laws because everyone would live a simple life, sharing all they had with everyone else. One day, Marx hoped the whole world would be Communist.

Not surprisingly, many poor ordinary workers were attracted to this theory. A Communist life sounded a lot better than the one they had! In the 1800s, people in several countries rebelled against their rulers and tried to set up Communist countries – they all failed. Then, in 1917, ordinary Russians who believed in a Communist way of life rebelled against their king, Nicholas II. He was a tough king, keeping himself in power by harsh laws and severe punishments. Things became worse when Russia got involved in the Great War. The army suffered heavy defeats, there were massive food shortages and nearly two million soldiers were killed. The Russian Revolution of 1917 got rid of the king – he and his family were murdered a few years later – and replaced him with a Communist government – the first in the world.

▶ **Source A** The Communist flag. In 1924, Russia, together with the smaller countries it controlled, was renamed the Union of Soviet Socialist Republics (USSR). 'Soviet' is a Russian word for 'council' whilst 'Socialist' is another word for 'Communist'. The flag tells a story: after the Revolution (red background), the power (golden star) is in the hands of the workers in industry (golden hammer) and agriculture (golden sickle). However, power was really in the hands of Joseph Stalin, the leader of the Communist Party!

Golden star for power

Red for revolution

Golden hammer for industry

Golden sickle for agriculture

However, the Communists in Russia ran the country as a dictatorship – they *forced* people to be equal and share.

- No other political parties were allowed to exist, only the Communist Party.

- Newspapers, books, films and radio broadcasts were all controlled by the Communists. Any person who spoke out against this was an 'enemy of the state' and sent to prison (or executed). Millions of people 'disappeared' in Communist Russia.

- Nobody was allowed to have any open religious beliefs. Only the Communist way of life was to be worshipped.

- All work, housing, health care and education was controlled by the Communists. Jobs, houses, hospitals and schools were provided for all Russians. The state owned everything ... and provided for everyone.

For many Russians, this was an ideal way of life. Everything was provided for them so long as they were prepared to work ... and not complain! However, Communism frightened people in other countries, particularly the rich factory owners, wealthy landowners, bankers, merchants and businessmen who didn't want to share any of their hard earned wealth – they'd worked too hard for it! Anyone with royal blood in their veins was worried too – kings, queens, princes, princesses, dukes and duchesses had seen what had happened to the Russian Royal family. They didn't want Communism spreading to their country.

As the years passed, fear of Communism in most other countries grew and grew and Russia became more and more isolated.

! WISE UP WORDS

Fascist   Fascism   Communist
Communism

A FASCIST DICTATORSHIP

CASE STUDY 2: ITALY

Italy had fought on the winning side in the Great War. 600 000 Italians had died and the government hoped Italy would be rewarded with land from the losing countries. They were wrong – Italy got hardly any land at all.

By 1919, Italy was in a bit of a mess – one in ten Italians were unemployed, food prices were high and riots were common. Bands of ex-soldiers were roaming the country stealing and murdering too! As you can imagine, richer Italians were afraid of these bandits. They were also afraid that those 'share-and-share-alike' Communists might take over too.

Increasingly, Italians turned to a young politician called Benito Mussolini, an ex-soldier and teacher! Mussolini promised to bring discipline back to Italy ... at a price! He called this theory 'Fascism' and formed the Fascist Party in 1919.

The basic idea of Fascism was that the government should control the whole of a person's life (that's right, it's another type of dictatorship!). The government controls education, newspapers, films and radio, even sport. People are still free to run their own businesses and make money, but there are tight controls on the workers – they can't go on strike, for example. In return, Mussolini and his Fascist Party would 'look after' Italy. They would build roads and railways, which would give people jobs. Poor people would be given money to help them find work and the army would be increased in size in order to protect Italy's borders. The Fascists would aim to make Italy great again and amongst the elite nations of the world. To a Fascist, the theory of Communism was wrong; all people were not equal, some were better than others. According to the Fascists, men were better than women, some races and nations better than others.

By 1922, Mussolini announced he was marching to Rome to take over. His supporters, all dressed in black uniforms, marched with him. The King of Italy gave in and made Mussolini Italy's new Prime Minister. Italy was now a dictatorship – Mussolini made all the laws, opposition to him was forbidden and opponents were beaten up or murdered.

By 1923, Mussolini's efforts to restore Italy had attracted the attention of a 34-year-old up-and-coming politician who was living in Germany. His name was Adolf Hitler. Perhaps Mussolini's ideas could work in Germany too!

▶ **Source B** Italy's Fascist flag. The eagle is a traditional symbol of power and alertness, whilst the bundle the eagle is clutching is called a 'fasces'. The bundle of sticks represents strength in number, unity and law – the axe symbolises power.

Source C Mussolini, Italy's Fascist leader, mounted huge displays, with uniforms and special salutes. Here he is pictured after a speech that encouraged university students to join the army. The words mean 'believe', 'obey' and 'fight'. Mussolini once said, 'A minute on the battlefield is worth a life time of peace ... better to live one day like a lion than a hundred years like a sheep'.

CREDERE

OBBEDIRE
COMBATTERE

WORK

1 Match up the names on the left with the correct description on the right.

Fascism — The Fascist leader of Italy who took control in 1922.

Communism — A German, living in London, who first thought up the theory of Communism.

Mussolini — From 1922, this was the new name for Russia and the areas it controlled.

USSR — One of the symbols of Italy's Fascist Party.

Karl Marx — A political system where all people are equal and all property and business is owned by the state and run for the benefit of all.

Fasces — A political system where the government controls all aspects of people's lives in an attempt to make the nation stronger than others.

2 a Find two similarities and two differences between the dictatorships of the USSR and Italy.

b Why were richer people across Europe worried about the spread of Communism?

c Why did Mussolini become popular in Italy after the end of the Great War?

3 a Draw a neat copy of the Communist flag in your book.

b Underneath, write a sentence or two about it.

c Draw a copy of the Fascist flag in your book.

d Underneath, write a sentence or two about it.

Adolf Hitler – choirboy, artist, tramp, soldier, politician

▶ What was Hitler's early life like?

▶ How did Hitler's early life influence him?

Adolf Hitler is one of the most **infamous** men ever to have lived. He is known mainly for his association with World War Two and his hatred of the Jews. But his time as leader of Germany only covers the last 12 years of his life! What about his early life? What was he like as a young man? How and why did he get involved in politics? And why was this Austrian (yes, he wasn't German at all) chosen to be Germany's leader in 1933?

Choirboy

▼ **Source A** Hitler (circled) at school in 1899, aged ten. He was in the local church choir for five years.

Adolf Hitler was born in 1889 in Braunau, a small town in Austria. His dad was a hard-drinking bully who worked as a postman. He died when Hitler was 14. His mum spoiled Hitler and insisted he went to a respectable school in order to get good grades and a well-paid job. But he failed his examinations and left school at 16. For the next two years he read books, listened to music and painted pictures. His mum died when he was 17. After her death, he left his home town and travelled to Vienna, the capital city of Austria, looking for work.

▼ **Source B** One of Hitler's teachers said this about him after he left school (from 'The Twentieth Century', by J D Clare, 1993)

'He always wanted his own way. He was boastful, bad-tempered and lazy... He ignored advice and got angry if he was told off.'

Artist and tramp

In 1907, Hitler arrived in Vienna hoping to 'make it big' as an artist. He tried to get into the Vienna Art Academy, one of Europe's best art colleges, but failed to pass the entrance exam. Without any qualifications, he ended up living in a hostel for tramps.

For the next five years, Hitler earned money any way he could – cleaning windows, painting houses, drawing and selling postcards in the street. He grew to hate people of foreign races, particularly rich Jewish people. He felt that foreigners were ruining Austria by taking over all the jobs and introducing their way of life.

▼ **Source C** Another tramp in the hostel remembers Hitler's arrival (from 'Weimar Germany', by Josh Brooman, 1985)

'On the very first day there sat next to the bed that had been given to me a man who had nothing on except an old torn pair of trousers – Hitler. His clothes were being cleaned of lice, since for days he had been wandering about without a roof over his head.'

◀ **Source D** Hitler could draw buildings well ... but struggled to draw people. This picture by Hitler shows why he failed to get into the Vienna Art Academy.

Soldier

Hitler left Austria in 1913 to avoid being called into the army. He went to live in Munich, Germany. When the Great War started in 1914, he decided to be a soldier after all and volunteered to join the German army.

Hitler was in hospital when the war ended, temporarily blinded in a gas attack. He wrote that he buried his head in his pillow and cried when he heard the news. He blamed Germany's surrender on weak politicians ... and, of course, the Jews!

▼ **Source E** Hitler (on the left) in the trenches in 1916. He worked all through the war as a messenger in the trenches. It was a dangerous job – he was wounded badly several times, once when a piece of metal sliced through his cheek. He nearly died.

▼ **Source F** A report of Hitler by his commanding officer during the Great War. The Iron Cross was the highest medal awarded in the German army.

Report on Lance Corporal Hitler, Third Company (volunteers)

Hitler has been with the regiment since 1914 and has fought splendidly in all the battles in which he has taken part.

As a messenger, he was always ready to carry messages in the most difficult positions at great risk to his own life.

He received the Iron Cross (Second Class) on 2 December 1914 and I now feel he is worthy of receiving the Iron Cross (First Class).

▼ **Source G** Hitler's membership card for the German Workers' Party. Hitler always claimed he was the seventh member, but his card shows that he was member number 555. Some historians say that the party started numbering at 500 to make it look like they had more members.

▼ **Source H** A comment made by a member of the German Workers' Party when they first heard Hitler speak.

'My God! He's got a big gob. We could make good use of him.'

Politician

Hitler stayed in the army after the war, working as a V-man, spying on new political groups to see if they were dangerous. One group he investigated wasn't dangerous at all – they had few members and funds of only 7.5 marks – about £4. They were called the German Workers' Party.

After a few months, Hitler decided to join this new political party. He liked many of its ideas and became member number 555. Before long, he was making speeches and writing articles to local newspapers about the party's beliefs and ideas for a better Germany. By 1921, Hitler was running the party – and he changed its name to the National Socialist German Workers' Party – or Nazi Party for short!

(!) **WISE UP WORD**

infamous

WORK

1 Make a timeline of events in Hitler's life up to 1921. You should be able to find at least ten important events on these pages. The first event in his life has been started for you:

1889: Born in Braunau, a small town in Austria. His father…

2 Answer the following questions in full sentences.

a Why did Hitler fail to get a place in the Vienna Art Academy?

b Whilst living in Vienna, why did Hitler begin to hate foreigners, especially Jews?

c In your opinion, was Hitler a good soldier? Give reasons for your answer.

d What was a V-man?

e Why do you think Hitler always claimed he was the seventh member of the German Workers' Party when his membership card said he was member number 555?

Why were the Nazis so popular?

▸ What tactics did the Nazis use to win votes?

▸ Why did people vote for Hitler?

In 1921, Hitler took over a small political party called the German Workers' Party. He renamed it the National Socialist German Workers' Party – or Nazi Party for short. It only had a few members and hardly any money. Twelve years later, the Nazis were the largest political party in Germany and Hitler was the nation's **Chancellor** or Prime Minister.

So what made Hitler so popular? How did he rise so quickly from the leader of a small political party ... to the leader of a nation?

Hitler criticised the Treaty of Versailles

Germany was in a mess when Hitler took over the Nazi Party. Harvests were poor and unemployment was high. Added to this was the fact that millions of Germans felt humiliated by the Treaty of Versailles. The winning countries had taken away land (15%) and money (they wanted £7 billion!) from Germany at the end of the Great War ... and blamed the Germans for starting it. Germans also felt vulnerable to attack because they were forced to reduce their army and have no air force, submarines or tanks at all – and only a tiny navy. As soon as he took over the Nazi Party, Hitler started to criticise the Treaty of Versailles. He said it was unfair and any land taken away from Germany must be returned. He said the French, who many Germans thought were responsible for the Treaty being so tough, must be destroyed!

Hitler's ideas made him popular

Hitler's views about the Treaty of Versailles made him popular and by 1923 the Nazi Party had over 50 000 members. Hitler even had his own private army of thugs called **storm troopers**, who went around beating people up who criticised him.

In 1923, Hitler felt confident enough to try to take over Germany. He tried to start a revolution in Munich, one of Germany's major cities, hoping it would spread to other places. It failed and Hitler was put in prison for treason. Whilst in prison, he wrote a book about his life and ideas called *Mein Kampf* – My Struggle. When Hitler was released in 1924 (for good behaviour), his book started to get him a reputation as a man whose ideas might be able to put Germany 'on the right track' again.

▾ **Source A** A few of Hitler's ideas

Mein Kampf

- The Treaty of Versailles was unfair and land taken away from Germany must be returned.

- All Germans, including those living in other countries, must be united under one leader — a dictator. Germany needs more land to feed and house this population.

- Humans are divided into races. Some races are better than others. The best races are 'pure' ones that haven't interbred with others. The Germans, who belong to a pure 'master race' called the **Aryans**, must keep themselves pure.

- Jews are the biggest threat to German purity. They are trying to take over the world and must be destroyed.

- Germany must build up its weapons in order to be a great nation once more.

11

Hitler knew the value of good publicity

Hitler divided Germany into districts and gave loyal
followers the job of spreading Nazi ideas throughout the
country. There were Nazi clubs for young boys, girls,
students and teachers. The Nazis bought eight
newspapers and printed millions of posters and leaflets to
get their message across. Hitler himself took part in
fabulous parades where he made passionate speeches in
important towns all over Germany (see **Source B**). Hitler
even chose an old religious symbol (which actually means
well being) to become the emblem of the Nazi Party. He
felt it was an eye-catching image which was easy to
remember and easy to draw. By the end of 1928, over
100 000 Germans belonged to the Nazi Party.

▼ **Source C** The Nazi flag. The symbol in the centre is
known as the 'crooked cross' or the **swastika**. It
became Germany's official symbol in 1935.

▼ **Source B** A Nazi parade in 1927. The Nazis had
their own salute (the raised arm) to acknowledge each
other.

Hitler was a brilliant speaker

Hitler held huge public meetings or **mass rallies** to tell people of his ideas for a better Germany. Magnificent marching displays and loud music were later accompanied by a powerful speech. His booming voice, hypnotic eyes and fearful temper thrilled his audiences.

> ▼ **Source D** Hitler made a film of himself practising a speech in 1922. One expert calculated that the frequency of an angry man's voice is 200 vibrations per second. The frequency of Hitler's *normal* speaking voice was 228 vibrations per second. One historian described his voice as 'an assault on the eardrums'.

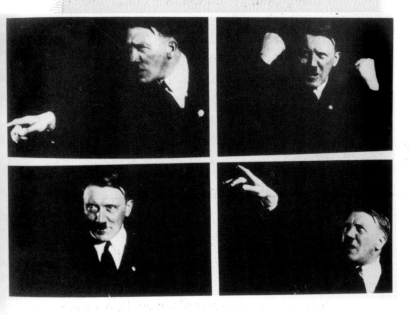

> ▼ **Source E** Otto Strasser, a German, wrote this after hearing Hitler speak. Strasser hated Hitler but recognised his excellent speaking skills.

'He is ... one of the greatest speakers of the century. Adolf Hitler enters a hall. He sniffs the air. For a minute he gropes, feels his way, senses the atmosphere. Suddenly he bursts forward. His words go like an arrow to his target, he touches each private wound on the raw ... telling it what it most wants to hear.'

Hitler was lucky

Over the years, many historians have argued that Hitler was in the right place at the right time. What do you think?

By 1928, Hitler and the Nazis were very well known ... but they were still only the eighth largest political party in Germany. Then, in 1929, world trade began to slow down. This means that countries stopped buying and selling to each other. German factories closed and people started to lose their jobs (see **Source F**). Hitler took advantage of this and started to promise solutions to all Germany's problems. 'Vote for me' was Hitler's message, 'and I'll provide you with work and bread'. As more and more people lost their jobs, the Nazis got more and more votes. By 1932, the Nazis were the largest political party – and Hitler became Chancellor (Prime Minister) of Germany in January 1933.

> ▼ **Source F** Written by a modern historian

'America had grown rich after the Great War. Their factories had done well selling goods such as cars, fridges, radios and watches in America and all over the world. Some Americans had money to spare and bought shares in companies and businesses hoping to make a profit. Some borrowed money from banks in order to join in this 'share-buying craze'. In October 1929, things started to go wrong. Many Americans hadn't made as much as they'd hoped from their shares. They decided to sell them ... fast. But the more they sold, the more the price dropped (try selling something that no one wants!). Millions of people couldn't sell the shares for as much as they'd paid for them. Some couldn't pay the banks back either. Soon many Americans couldn't afford to buy goods – as a result, firms went out of business and millions lost their jobs. Americans couldn't buy any foreign goods either ... including those from Germany. Soon German factories had to close down and Germans lost their jobs. We call this world slump in trade The Great Depression ... and Germany, like America, Britain and many other countries, was hit very hard.'

▼ **Source G** The relationship between unemployment and votes for the Nazis. The unemployed voted for Hitler because he promised jobs; ex-soldiers voted for him because he promised to build up Germany's armed services again; businessmen voted for him because they hoped to make money when he built tanks, aeroplanes, roads and railways to make Germany great again. He even got rich people to vote for him – Hitler promised to destroy Communism (he didn't think everyone was equal!) so the rich were happy they wouldn't have to divide up their wealth!

Year	Number of unemployed	Number of votes for the Nazis
1928	0.8m	1.8m
1929	2.8m	2.0m
1930	3.2m	4.7m
1931	4.9m	7.5m
1932	6.0m	11.7m
1933	6.5m	17.0m

▼ **Source H** A Nazi election poster of 1932. The writing means 'Our last hope: HITLER'. Who do you think this poster was aimed at?

Unsere letzte Hoffnung: HITLER

WORK

1 a Imagine you are one of these people, living in Germany in January 1933:
   i)   an unemployed person who has spent many years without a job;
   ii) an old soldier who fought in the Great War;
   iii) a businessman or woman;
   iv) a young person who has just left university and is looking for a job.

A friend from Britain has written to you asking about your new Chancellor, Adolf Hitler. They are interested to know:

   • A bit about his past – what's his history and how did he get into politics?
   • Why he's so popular – who's voting for him and why?
   • What he's promised the German people – what are his views and ideas for the future?
   • What sort of leader he might be – have you heard him speak or seen any of the publicity he has generated?
   • Whether you voted for him – if so, what reasons will you give your friend for doing so? If you didn't vote for Hitler, why not?

You should plan your letter carefully and write a draft version first. Set your letter out properly as if you were writing a real letter to a relative or pen pal.
Remember to try to imagine that you are one of the four people mentioned at the start of the question. Try to think of the way they would answer your friend's questions.

   b Compare your letter with someone else in the class who has pretended to be a different person. In what ways are the letters similar or different? Have you both got similar reasons for voting (or not voting) for Hitler?

2 a Draw the swastika flag in your book.
   b Write down at least three facts about it.

Life in Nazi Germany

AIMS

▶ How did the Nazis build a racist society?
▶ What was it like to be young in Nazi Germany?
▶ How did life change for women and the family?

Adolf Hitler was asked to become Chancellor by the President of Germany, Paul von Hindenburg. At this time, the President was the most powerful man in Germany and the Chancellor was his chief minister. When President Hindenburg died one year later, Hitler made himself both Chancellor AND President. He started to call himself **Führer** (supreme leader) and immediately got all members of the army to swear an oath (promise) of loyalty to him.

'I swear by God that by this sacred oath I will give complete obedience to the Führer Adolf Hitler ... and am ready as a brave soldier to risk my life at any time for him.'

▲ **Source A** The Oath of Loyalty, 1934. Note that the promise is made to Hitler, not Germany. Why do you think Hitler felt this oath was one of his first priorities?

Hitler quickly started to change things. Having worked so hard to get into power, he was determined to stay there. His secret police force, the dreaded **Gestapo**, hunted out anyone who might be against Hitler. They had the power to arrest and imprison people without trial and set up a web of informers who would report any 'moaners' to them. Children were encouraged to report their parents or teachers if they spoke out against the Führer and, by 1935, every block of flats or housing estate had a 'local ruler' who listened for negative comments. By 1939, there were well over 100 000 people in prison for 'anti-Hitler crimes' ... they were known as Enemies of the State.

▼ **Source B** Part of a Nazi press release from 1934. 'Culling' means to kill or remove any unwanted people.

'The Nazi government must have total control over every aspect of life. Government will be in the hands of one person, a genius, a hero, with total responsibility for culling on behalf of a pure race in the national interest.'

Who was on Hitler's hate list?

Hitler was determined to crush anyone who didn't fully support him. He once declared that any opponents would 'have their skulls bashed in'. However, most of Hitler's hatred was based on race. He believed that mankind was divided into races and some races were better or superior to others. He felt that superior races (like the Germans) had the right to dominate 'inferior' races, such as Jews, gypsies, Slavs (such as Russians) and black people.

People who were disabled in any way or mentally impaired were also targets for Hitler because they damaged the purity of the German race. Hitler thought these people should be eliminated so their illnesses and disabilities could not pass on to their children. 300 000 men and women were compulsorily **sterilised** in families with **hereditary** illnesses; 720 000 mentally ill people were gassed and 5 000 mentally impaired babies killed.

▼ **Source C** Based on an interview with a former inmate of one of Hitler's prisons. They were known as **concentration camps**.

'The prisons were full. Tramps, prostitutes and beggars were a common sight, but there were other prisoners too. Anyone who refused to join the army was sent to prison and so were people who'd been a member of any other political party except the Nazis. Trade union leaders were also inside and I once met a woman who had been reported for telling a joke at the Führer's expense. Another favourite tactic of the Gestapo was to accuse a man or woman of being homosexual — there were many in prison accused of this "crime".'

Source D These two signs were a common sight in Germany in the 1930s

> **JEWS ENTER THIS TOWN AT THEIR OWN RISK**

> **BATHING PROHIBITED TO DOGS AND JEWS**

HUNGRY FOR MORE? Hold a class discussion. If the people of Britain elected a Prime Minister with similar views to Hitler, would people in other countries have the right to remove him from power? Some people in the class should prepare a case 'for', and others in the class should prepare a case 'against' countries having the right to stop Britain's PM.

LAWS AGAINST JEWS, 1933–1939

March 1933 All Jewish lawyers and judges sacked.

April 1933 All Jews banned from any sports clubs. All Jewish teachers sacked.

September 1933 'Race studies' introduced in German schools.

January 1934 All Jewish shops marked with a yellow star of David – a symbol of the Jewish religion – or the word *Juden* (German for 'Jew'). Soldiers to stand outside shops turning people away.

September 1935 Jews not allowed to vote. Marriages between Jews and non-Jews banned.

January 1936 No Jew allowed to own any electrical equipment (including cameras), bicycles, typewriters or music records.

July 1938 Jewish doctors sacked.

August 1938 Male Jews must add the name 'Israel' and female Jews must add the name 'Sara' to their first names.

November 1938 Jewish children banned from German schools.

December 1938 Jewish and non-Jewish children forbidden to play together. Jews banned from using swimming pools.

April 1939 Jews can be evicted from their homes for no reason.

September 1939 Jews no longer allowed out of their homes between 8:00pm and 6:00am.

Source E Each of these laws was designed to make life more and more uncomfortable for German Jews. Hitler saw them as an inferior race that cared more about themselves than the greatness of Germany. There were approximately 500 000 Jews in Germany in 1934 (about 1% of the population). By the time Hitler stopped Jews from leaving the country (1941), nearly 80% had already left for new lives in other places.

Source F This humiliating photograph of a married couple was taken in 1933. It shows an Aryan woman and a Jewish man being bullied by the Nazis. The woman's sign reads 'I live with a pig and only go with Jews'. Her husband's sign reads 'Instead of Jews, I only take young German girls to my room'.

WORK

1 Write a sentence or two to explain the following words: Führer • Gestapo • concentration camp • sterilisation

2 Look at **Source E**.

a Write down five laws or policies that made life uncomfortable or difficult for German Jews.

b Next to each of your choices, explain why you think it was introduced by the Nazis. One has been done for you:

January 1934: Soldiers stood outside Jewish shops and told people not to shop there. I think this was introduced to ruin Jewish businesses – if they had to close their shops, they might leave Germany altogether.

Why were the young so important to Hitler?

	Lesson 1	Lesson 2	Lesson 3	Dinner	Lesson 4	Lesson 5	Lesson 6
BOYS	German	History/ Geography	Eugenics/ Nazi theory	Sport and music clubs	Physics and Chemistry	PE: boxing, football and marching	Maths
GIRLS	German	History/ Geography	Eugenics/ Nazi theory		Biology/ health and sex education	Cookery	Maths

▲ **Source G** A typical timetable for a day's education at a mixed school in Berlin, 1936. **Eugenics** is the scientific study of how to improve races. What major differences do you notice about the education process for the different sexes?

▼ **Source H** Youngsters were indoctrinated (brainwashed) to think like Nazis. Textbooks were rewritten to get across the Nazi message. Even teachers had to belong to the German Nazi Teachers' League and were made to put across Nazi ideas in their lessons – or face the sack. These questions are adapted and translated from a German textbook during the Nazi period.

Question 46:
The Jews are aliens in Germany. In 1933, there were 66 060 000 people living in Germany. Of this total, 499 862 were Jews. What is the percentage of aliens in Germany?

Question 52:
A bomber aircraft on take off carries 144 bombs, each weighing ten kilos. The aircraft bombs a town full of Jews. On take off with all bombs on board and a fuel tank containing 1000 kilos of fuel, the aircraft weighs about eight tons. When it returns from its victorious mission, there are still 230 kilos of fuel left. What is the weight of the aircraft when empty?

Question 67:
It costs, on average, four RM (reichmarks) a day to keep a cripple or a mentally ill person in hospital. There are currently 300 000 mentally ill, lunatics and so on in Germany's hospitals. How much would the German government save if they got rid of all these people?

Hitler took great trouble to make sure that young people were loyal to him and the Nazi Party.

He realised that in future he may have to call on these people to put up with hardships, to fight and perhaps die for him. It was important therefore that young people thought that Hitler and the Nazis were the best thing that ever happened to Germany. He needed young men who were 'as fast as a greyhound, as tough as leather and as hard as steel'. He wanted tough, strong, practical girls too ... but for an entirely different reason – they were to be the wives and mothers of a future generation of soldiers.

▼ **Source I** A picture from a German school textbook in 1935. Children were taught to recognise Jews at a glance. Look for: i) the way the Jewish children and adult (on the left) are drawn. Why have they been drawn this way? ii) the reaction of the other children to the Jews' departure; iii) the Jewish boy on the right pulling another child's hair – why has this been included?

▼ **Source J** Outside school, young people had to belong to the Hitler Youth Organisation. From the ages of 6 to 18, boys and girls spent a few evenings a week and several weekends a year learning new skills and being taught how to show their loyalty to Hitler. Boys tended to learn military skills (model making, shooting practice and hiking) whilst girls learned about cookery, housework and motherhood. In this photograph, Hitler is smiling at a six-year-old member of the Hitler Youth Organisation in full uniform. Why do you think this was a valuable photograph to the Nazis and shown all over Germany?

1) **Complete the following lessons:**
  i) Life of Hitler
  ii) Germans abroad
  iii) Germany's rightful place in the world
  iv) National holidays of the German people
  v) Five flag oaths
  vi) Six Hitler Youth songs

2) **Complete the following athletic tests:**
  i) Run 60 metres in 10 seconds
  ii) Long jump 3.25 metres
  iii) Throw a small leather ball 35 metres
  iv) Pull up on a bar twice
  v) Somersault backwards twice
  vi) Swim 100 metres

3) **Hiking and camping tests:**
  i) A day's hike of 15 kilometres
  ii) Camp in a tent for three days
  iii) Put up a two-man tent and take part in putting up a twelve-man tent
  iv) Make a cooking pit and find water for cooking
  v) Know the names of the most important trees
  vi) Use the stars to find your place on a map

4) **Target practice:**
  Hit a bull's eye on a target at a distance of eight metres with an air gun

▲ **Source K** An extract from the guidebook of the Hitler Youth Organisation. It describes what a 10- to 14-year-old boy had to do to get an 'Achievement Award'. Would you be tough enough?

WORK

1 Why do you think Hitler and the Nazis put so much effort into organising the lives of young people?

2 Look at **Source G**.
  a In what ways is this timetable different to school timetables today?
  b Why do you think boys and girls were taught different things?
  c What is 'eugenics' and why do you think the Nazis put this on every school's timetable?

3 Look at **Source H**.
  a In what ways are these questions different to ones that appear in your maths books today?
  b Why do you think questions like these appeared in German textbooks?

4 a Draw up two posters, both showing how the Nazis were trying to organise the lives of young people. One poster should be aimed at the young people themselves. The other should be for their parents.
  b In what ways are the posters different?

75

Was it a sexist society?

In Hitler's eyes, a woman's most important job was to have children – lots of them, especially boys.

PAUSE FOR THOUGHT

Why do you think Hitler wanted so many boys?

Women were encouraged to stay at home and be good wives and mothers. Going out and getting qualifications and a professional job was frowned upon as it might get in the way of producing lots of babies. Loans were given to newly married couples – the equivalent of a year's wages – to encourage them to have children. On the birth of a first child, they could keep a quarter of the money. On the birth of another they could keep the second quarter. They could keep the third quarter on the birth of a third child and keep the lot on the birth of a fourth. Every year, on 12 August, the birthday of Hitler's mother, the Motherhood Medal was awarded to women who had the most children.

▼ **Source M** A Nazi law written in 1943. It never came into effect.

'All single and married women up to the age of 35 who do not already have four children should produce four children by racially pure German men. Whether or not these men are married is not important. Every family that already has four children must set the husband free for this action.'

How did Hitler please ordinary Germans?

The vast majority of ordinary Germans did well out of Hitler's rule between 1933 and 1939. Right from the start, he said he would provide work, bread and restore national pride. He said he would make sure that Germany regained its rightful place in the world.

In 1933, there were six million people out of work, but this figure had reduced to 200 000 by 1938. The Nazis provided work by building roads, schools, hospitals, railways ... and by making the army bigger and building tanks, fighter planes and battleships. Hitler started to get back land Germany had lost after its defeat in the Great War and many Germans felt a sense of pride in this. If the German people were prepared to ignore some of the crueller things happening to a minority of people, and not complain too loudly, it seemed that life was better under Hitler's leadership.

◄ **Source L** A Nazi poster of 1937 showing what Nazis thought a woman's role in life should be. Look for: i) the plain, simple image of a woman breastfeeding her baby. Make up and wearing trousers were frowned upon by the Nazis. Permed or dyed hair was banned and slimming was discouraged because it was not thought to be good for childbearing; ii) her husband working on the land, providing for Germany whilst his wife takes care of things at home; iii) the church in the background. Hitler thought the ideal woman should stick to the 'three Ks' – *Kinder*, *Kirche* and *Kuche* (children, church and cooking).

▼ **Source N** The 'People's Car' or Volkswagen was launched in 1938. The car, designed by Ferdinand Porsche, was meant to 'look like a beetle' because Hitler admired this insect's fighting nature. The text on this advert reads 'five marks a week is all you have to save if you want to drive your own car'. Millions started to save for their 'beetle' but the whole scheme was a swindle. Not one customer received their car – the money was used to build weapons! Why do you think no one complained about not receiving their cars?

5 Mark die Woche musst Du sparen- willst Du in signen Wagen fahren!

▼ **Source O** The feelings of a man who attended a Nazi rally in 1937.

'I don't know how to describe the emotions that swept over me as I heard Adolf Hitler ... when he spoke of the disgrace of Germany I was ready to spring on any enemy ... I forgot everything but Hitler. Then, glancing around, I saw that the thousands around me were drawn to him like a magnet as well.'

FACT: ▶ Mastermind

▶ Hitler was determined to control the way people thought. The Nazis controlled all newspapers, films, radio, plays, cinema and books – and made sure they put across Nazi ideas. One of Hitler's most trusted friends, Doctor Joseph Goebbels, was put in charge of propaganda and **censorship**. He became a master of mind control. He had loud speakers placed on all city streets so that people could hear Hitler's speeches when they were doing their shopping and ordered all books written by Jews or Communists to be destroyed. He banned jazz music because it was played mainly by black American musicians and even had a war film destroyed because it showed a drunk German sailor. He even introduced the death penalty for telling an anti-Hitler joke!

▼ **Source P** Adapted from 'Hitler's Germany', by Josh Brooman, 1991

'[The Nazis] drew up massive leisure programmes for working people. The biggest programme provided workers with cheap holidays ... a cruise to the Canary Islands, for example, cost 62 marks, the equivalent of two weeks' wages. Although most workers could afford this, it was only loyal and hardworking members of the Nazi Party who were given places on the cruise liners. For those who could not get a place on a cruise ship, there were walking holidays ... skiing holidays ... two weeks in Switzerland ... or a tour of Italy. [The Nazis arranged] sports matches ... outings to the theatre and the opera. It had its own symphony orchestra, which toured the country playing music in areas not usually visited by orchestras. It laid on evening classes for adults.'

(!) WISE UP WORDS

Führer   Gestapo   concentration camps
sterilised   hereditary   eugenics
indoctrinated   censorship

WORK

1 Read **Source M**. In your own words, explain how this law tried to encourage Germans to have more children.

2 a How did Hitler create jobs?
  b What effect do you think the creation of lots of jobs had on his popularity?

3 a In 1937, a leading Nazi said: 'The only people who have a private life in Germany today are those who are asleep.' Use the information and sources on pages 72 to 77 to give examples of how people's private lives were affected by the Nazis.
  b Why do you think Hitler put someone in charge of propaganda and censorship?
  c Why do you think he gave the job to one of his most trusted friends?

The Olympic Games, 1936

▶ How did the Nazis try to use the 1936 Olympic Games to show the superiority of the German way of life?

▶ Were Hitler's efforts rewarded with success?

For many years, the Olympic Games have been one of the most exciting and popular spectacles on the sports calendar. Countries from all over the world spend millions of pounds trying to win the right to host the Olympics in one of their nations' cities. Not only are the Olympics a chance for a country to make money (sponsorship, TV deals and so on), they are an opportunity to show the world what a fantastic place the host nation is. In 1936, the Olympics were due to be held in Berlin, Germany's capital city. Hitler decided to deliberately use them to show the world how splendid Nazi Germany was. So were the Berlin Olympics of 1936 a Nazi success story? Did the Olympics show the world how wonderful the Nazis were? And did everything go exactly to plan?

▼ **Source A** An artist's impression of the poster for the Olympic Games. The five rings represent the five major continents of the world that send athletes to compete – Europe, Asia, Africa, the Americas (North and South) and Oceania.

FACT: ▶ Modern technology

▶ A new stadium to hold 100 000 people was built which used the most modern electric lighting and most advanced 'photo finish' equipment ever made. The stadium had the largest stop clock ever built and television cameras were used to record all the action for the first time. Hitler used every opportunity to show as many swastika flags as he could. Why do you think he did this?

▼ **Source B** From an American book written about Nazi Germany in 1959 (quoted in 'Weimar and Nazi Germany', by Fiona Reynoldson, 1996)

'The Olympic Games were held in Berlin in August 1936. The signs saying "Jews not welcome" were quietly taken down from shops and hotels, the **persecution** of the Jews halted for a time and the country put on its best behaviour.'

(!) **WISE UP WORD**

persecution

▼ **Source C** From a textbook written by a modern historian (from 'GCSE Modern World History', by Ben Walsh, 1996). Joseph Goebbels was put in charge of the organisation of the Games by Hitler himself.

'With guests and competitors from 49 countries coming into the heart of Nazi Germany, it was going to take all Goebbels' talents to show that Germany was a modern, civilised and successful nation. No expense was spared. When the Games opened, the visitors were duly amazed at the scale of the stadium, the wonderful facilities and the efficiency of the organisation. However, they were also struck by, and in some cases appalled by, the almost fanatical devotion of the people to Hitler and the ... presence of ... soldiers who were patrolling or standing guard everywhere.'

▼ **Source D** The start of the 100-metre sprint final, won by black American athlete Jesse Owens (nearest the camera) in a world record time.

To Hitler's great joy, the German Olympic squad came top of the medal table, way ahead of all other countries. This, Hitler claimed, showed how talented and strong the German race was and how it was superior to other 'inferior' races. However, to Hitler's great dismay, a black American athlete named Jesse Owens became the star of the games. He won four gold medals (100- and 200-metre sprints, long jump and 4 x 100-metre relay), breaking many world records in the process. So much for Hitler's race theories about white 'Aryan' Germans being fitter, stronger and faster than all others. Not surprisingly, Hitler refused to present Owens with his medals, as this would have meant shaking hands with a black champion.

WORK

1 a Why was Hitler keen for Nazi Germany to host the 1936 Olympic Games?

   b Imagine you had gone to the opening ceremony of the 1936 Olympic Games. Do you think you would have been impressed by what you'd have seen? Give reasons for your answer.

2 Look at **Source B**.

   a Why do you think the Nazis stopped picking on Jews during the Games?

   b The German Olympic team included one Jewish athlete. Why do you think he was included in the squad?

3 Look at **Source C**. According to the writer, what two things may have 'appalled' some of the visitors to the Games?

4 a What was Jesse Owens' achievement at the 1936 Berlin Olympics?

   b Why do you think Hitler refused to shake hands with him? Can you explain his behaviour?

   c What do you think about Hitler's behaviour?

5 In your opinion, were the 1936 Olympic Games a Nazi success or not?

Have you been learning?

Task 1 Votes for women

Read the following 1910 newspaper report very carefully. It appeared the day after a 'Votes for Women' march in London had turned to violence.

120 ARRESTED

Suffragettes attack House of Commons

D I S G R A C E F U L   S C E N E S

Reckless women charge at police

True to their word, about 300 Suffragettes marched on the House of Commons yesterday and the scenes of violence were worse than any other of which they had been guilty. It was a picture of shameful recklessness. Never before have otherwise sensible women gone so far in forgetting their womanhood. One woman campaigner fell in the mud, to the disgust of decent men but to the delight of others. One obese Suffragette threw her untidy self against smiling policemen until she ran out of breath. A few more of the desperate pushed at the heroic police in rugby style until they were swung back by a powerful neck or waist grip. Arrests were only made in extreme cases and many women were sadly disappointed not to be taken into custody. Even so, 120 people were arrested, including some men.

a Who were the Suffragettes?

b Is this newspaper report biased for or against the Suffragettes? Quote any words or phrases that support your view.

c Rewrite the news article in an unbiased way, using the facts in the article.

d In what ways is your news report different from the original?

Task 2 Note making

Note making is an important skill. To do it successfully, you must pick out the key words in each sentence. The key words are the ones that are vital to the meaning. Without these words, the sentence makes no sense.

For example: The first day of the Battle of the Somme was a terrible day in British history – 20 000 British soldiers were killed and 35 000 were wounded.

The key words are: first day; Battle of the Somme; 20 000 British soldiers killed; 35 000 wounded.

a Now write down the key words in the following sentences about Hitler's early life. The key words are your notes.
  • Adolf Hitler was born in 1889 in Braunau, a small town in Austria.
  • His bullying father died when Hitler was 14 and his mother died when he was 17. He left school when he was 16 and dreamt of being a famous artist.
  • Hitler failed to get into the Vienna Art Academy and ended up living in a hostel for tramps. He earned money by cleaning windows, painting houses and selling postcards on the streets. He began to hate the rich Jews of Vienna.
  • He joined the army when the Great War started in 1914 and won medals for bravery as a trench messenger. By the time the war ended, he had managed to win the highest medal in the German army – the Iron Cross (First Class).
  • Hitler was temporarily blinded in a gas attack and was in hospital when the war ended. He blamed Germany's defeat on weak German politics and Jews! He hated the way Germany was punished after the war and decided to go into politics.
  • After the war ended, Hitler was given the job of spying on some of the many new German political parties. He went to a meeting of one called 'The German Workers' Party' and liked their ideas. He joined the party and was soon its leader.
  • Hitler changed the party's name to 'The National Socialist German Workers' Party' or 'Nazi Party' for short. They used the swastika as their emblem.

b Why not make notes on other topics you have studied?

Task 3 The Jews in Nazi Germany 1933–1939

Once in power, the Nazis quickly began to make life difficult for Germany's Jews. One of the first things they did was to organise a boycott of Jewish shops. This photograph of two Nazis pinning up a notice on a Jewish clothes shop was taken on 1 April 1933 – study it carefully and then answer the questions in full sentences.

a What is a 'boycott'?

b Why do you think the Nazis organised boycotts of Jewish shops?

c What do you think the poster might say?

d What effect do you think the poster might have had on the shoppers?

e What does the word 'persecute' mean?

f In what other ways did the Nazis persecute Jews up to 1939?

Task 4 What's missing?

a Using the clues, copy out the following names, labels or words from your studies so far. Some have missing vowels; others have missing consonants.

b Write a sentence or two explaining each name, label or word.

i) S _ f f r _ g _
(another word for vote)

ii) _ m _ l y D _ v _ s _ n
(Derby, 1913)

iii) _ a _ i _ _ o _ _ _ e o _ _ e
(British PM at the end of the Great War)

iv) T r _ _ t y _ f V _ r s _ _ l l _ s
(punished Germany)

v) _ e a _ u e o _ _ a _ i o _ _
(to prevent future wars)

vi) d _ m _ c r _ c y
(voting for leaders)

vii) _ i _ _ a _ o _ _ _ i _
(one leader, no right to vote)

viii) M _ s s _ l _ n _
(Italy's Fascist leader)

ix) _ o _ _ u _ i _ _
(USSR after 1922)

x) _ e i _ _ a _ _ _
(Hitler's book)

xi) _ _ a _ _ i _ a
(crooked cross)

xii) F _ h r _ r
(supreme leader)

xiii) G _ s t _ p _
(secret police)

xiv) _ i _ _ e _ _ o u _ _
(tough Nazi kids)

xv) _ e _ _ e O _ e _ _
(four gold medals)

81

Why was there another world war?

▶ How did World War Two begin?
▶ To what extent was it 'Hitler's War'?

Adolf Hitler, who became leader of Germany in 1933, was determined to make Germany great again. He had fought as a losing German soldier in the Great War of 1914–1918 and, like millions of Germans, was humiliated by the punishment Germany received at the end of the fighting (see **Source A**).

▼ **Source A** The agreement or treaty reached at the end of the Great War. Not surprisingly, most Germans hated it. Hitler swore revenge!

Treaty of Versailles

- The Great War is Germany's fault.

- The Germans must pay for the war … until 1988. The money will go to the British and French.

- Germany should only have a small army (100 000 men), a small navy (six battleships) and no submarines, air force or tanks.

- Germany must hand over huge areas of its land to the winners. Some of the land will be used to make new countries like Poland and Czechoslovakia.

- Germany must never unite with Austria ever again.

- No German soldiers can go into an area known as the Rhineland, a German region close to France.

Signed Britain, France, Italy, the USA and all other winners.

Hitler had three main aims in his dealings with other countries. Firstly, he wanted to do everything in his power to get all the land back that Germany lost after the Great War. He felt he would have to build up his army, navy and air force to do this. Despite the fact that this would mean breaking the rules laid down at the end of the Great War, Hitler was determined to ignore them and carry on regardless. Secondly, he wanted to join together anyone who spoke German into one big country. Finally, he wanted to make Germany bigger by taking land from other, weaker countries. He believed that true Germans were such a great and powerful race that they needed the extra living space (he called it 'Lebensraum') to reach their full potential.

Three days after becoming leader of Germany, Hitler told his military chiefs to start building up the army, navy and air force in secret. This was known as **rearmament**. By 1935, Hitler had dozens more aeroplanes and battleships than he was allowed … and thousands more soldiers! In late 1935, Hitler even told the world about his increased armed forces, but no one did anything. Some countries didn't want to stand up to Hitler for fear of starting another war, whilst others felt that Germany should be allowed to build up their armed forces if they wanted to. After all, they were only protecting themselves, weren't they?

▼ **Source B** A German postcard produced in 1935. The aim of this postcard was to persuade people that it was unfair that Germany was not allowed to build up its armed forces but all other countries around them were. Do you think Hitler had a point? The orange area around the River Rhine was the part where no German troops were allowed at all.

In 1936, Hitler broke the rules again by sending his soldiers into the Rhineland area of Germany. But his soldiers were not allowed anywhere near France, remember (see **Source A**)! Once again, no country stopped him – after all, he wasn't invading another country, just moving his soldiers around *within* his own, they thought!

Yet Hitler's aggressive moves worried some politicians. Winston Churchill, for example, made many speeches in Parliament about the need to stand up to Hitler. But Churchill was not Prime Minister at this time; just an ordinary MP ... and many people ignored him! But Hitler's actions were starting to make world news – so what would be his next daring move?

WORK

1 a Why did Hitler (and millions of other Germans) hate the Treaty of Versailles?

   b Explain how Hitler broke the Treaty of Versailles between 1933 and 1936.

   c Why did the leaders of some countries refuse to stand up to Hitler at this time?

2 Look at **Source B**.

   a How did the postcard try to persuade British people that the German armed forces had been reduced unfairly by the Treaty of Versailles?

   b Do you think the postcard helps to explain why Hitler wanted his army in the Rhineland?

In 1938, German troops marched into Austria, the country of Hitler's birth. Once again, Hitler had broken the rules laid down at the end of the Great War (see **Source A**). Once again, no country stopped him. After all, many Austrians *wanted* to be part of Germany … and Hitler was Austrian anyway!

By 1938, it seemed as if Hitler was unstoppable. His armed forces were getting stronger and he was demanding more land. He next turned his attention to the Sudetenland, a small area of Czechoslovakia that contained many people who spoke German as their first language (see **Source D**). Hitler told the world that he wanted this region. In September 1938, Neville Chamberlain, the British Prime Minister, visited Hitler in Germany to discuss Hitler's demands. The French leader attended the meeting too. On 29 September, the British and the French agreed to let Germany have the Sudetenland. The Czechoslovakian leaders were not even at the meeting, but went along with the more powerful countries' decision! Hitler said he was happy and the world breathed a sigh of relief. In Britain, Chamberlain was a hero (see **Source E**). He had even got Hitler to sign a piece of paper saying that he was satisfied with everything and didn't want anything else!

▼ **Source C** A photograph of the German invasion of Austria, March 1938.

▼ **Source D** A map of Europe in the 1930s

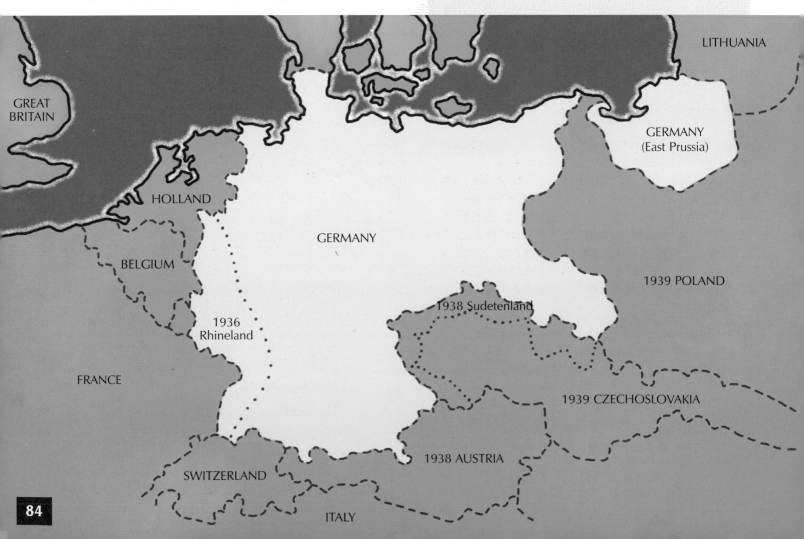

LITHUANIA

GREAT BRITAIN

GERMANY (East Prussia)

HOLLAND

GERMANY

BELGIUM

1939 POLAND

1936 Rhineland

1938 Sudetenland

FRANCE

1939 CZECHOSLOVAKIA

1938 AUSTRIA

SWITZERLAND

ITALY

▼ **Source E** An artist's interpretation of a British cartoon published in September 1938. What is the message of this cartoon? Use these questions to help you uncover the message:

- What problem is Chamberlain dealing with?
- What is Chamberlain doing to the world? And where is the world going?
- Where will the world end up without Chamberlain?
- Does the cartoon show him in a good or a bad way?

Neville Chamberlain, British PM

But all Hitler's promises were exposed as lies in March 1939 when his soldiers took over the rest of Czechoslovakia. It seemed that he wasn't satisfied with just the Sudetenland at all ... he wanted more and more. Suddenly, the countries of Europe realised that Hitler could never be trusted and prepared for war. They wondered if they would be next. Britain and France had had enough of letting Hitler get away with things (this was known as **appeasement**) and agreed to help Poland if Hitler invaded it.

Sure enough, Poland was next on Hitler's hit list. He threatened to invade in August 1939, but only after he made a clever alliance with the USSR. Hitler thought that the Russians might feel threatened if he continued to push his soldiers in their direction so he made a deal with Stalin, the Russian leader. A secret part of the deal said the Russians could have part of Poland if they let the Germans invade.

On 1 September 1939, German troops invaded Poland. Chamberlain decided that enough was enough. Two days later, on 3 September 1939, Britain declared war on Germany. France declared war too. Later that evening, Chamberlain went on the radio to tell the British public (see **Source F**).

▼ **Source F** Part of Chamberlain's speech on 3 September 1939

'This country is at war with Germany ... May God bless you all. It is evil things that we are fighting against – brute force, bad faith, injustice, oppression and persecution; and against that, I am certain that right will prevail [win].'

FACT: ▶ What happened next?

▶ Poland was defeated quickly. Hitler's troops then went on to invade Norway, Holland, Belgium and even France. On 10 May 1940, Winston Churchill, the man who had warned the world about Hitler, took over as the British Prime Minister. Hitler eventually invaded the USSR in June 1941 (so much for his alliance!) but was forced back in the winter after getting to within 60 miles of Russia's capital, Moscow! If you're hungry for more information on World War Two ... get researching!

WISE UP WORDS

rearmament   appeasement

WORK

1 Look at **Source C**. What does this photograph tell us about the feelings of ordinary Austrians when Hitler invaded in 1938? Give reasons for your answer.

2 Look at **Source E**.

a What is meant by the word 'appeasement'?

b How did Britain and France 'appease' Hitler in 1938?

c Do you think the cartoonist supported Chamberlain's actions or not? Give reasons for your answer. CLUE: Does he show the British Prime Minister in a positive way or not?

Who were the 'Few'?

> ► What was 'Operation Sealion'?
> ► Why was Britain not invaded on 15 September 1940?

Towards the end of 1940, posters like the one in **Source A** began to appear all over Britain. They featured five smiling fighter pilots and a famous quotation from Britain's Prime Minister, Winston Churchill. So why was this poster published? Why were the pilots smiling? And why did 'so many' people have to be thankful to 'so few'?

▼ **Source A** 'Never was so much owed by so many to so few' poster interpreted by an artist

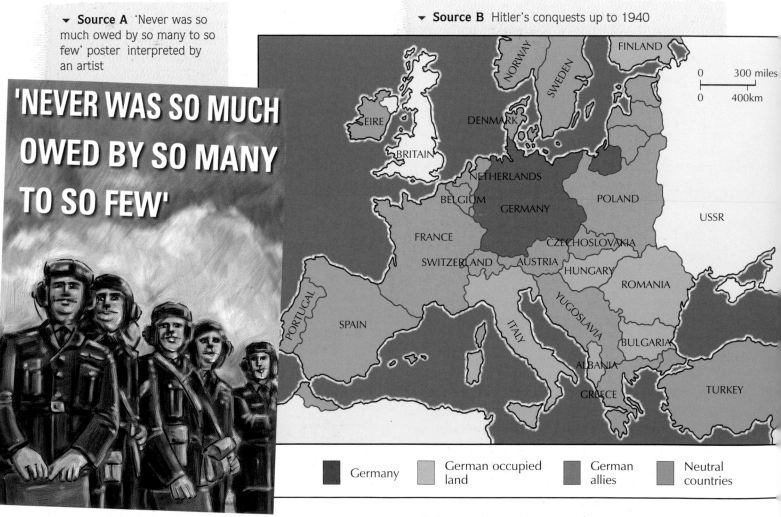

▼ **Source B** Hitler's conquests up to 1940

Germany | German occupied land | German allies | Neutral countries

By July 1940, Hitler was 'Master of Europe'. He was friendly with, or his armies had successfully invaded, most European countries (see **Source B**). Now only Britain and the USSR stood in his way ... and Britain was to be first on his hit list.

On 1 August 1940, Hitler signed top secret plans to begin the invasion of Britain. Code-named 'Operation Sealion', the aim was to get German soldiers onto British soil by 15 September. After that, German troops would move towards London and other major British cities with the goal of controlling the whole country by Christmas.

Source C A summary of Operation Sealion. The RAF was the Royal Air Force, the official title of Britain's air force.

TOP SECRET

GERMAN GOVERNMENT
TOP SECRET DIRECTIVE NO. 17, 1 AUGUST 1940

FROM: ADOLF HITLER

In order to establish the conditions necessary for the final conquest of Britain, I intend to step up the air and naval war more intensively.

i) From 6 August, German bombers should attack British airfields and destroy all the RAF's aircraft. These bombers should be protected by fighter aircraft.

ii) If Britain does not surrender after all her aircraft are destroyed, the German army, escorted by the German navy, will land on beaches between Folkestone and Brighton on 15 September.

The success of Operation Sealion hinged on the complete defeat of Britain's air force. Hitler believed that if the Luftwaffe (German Air Force) could win control of the skies, it would be far easier for German ships to transport soldiers over the English Channel to begin the land invasion of Britain. If the RAF was destroyed, British planes could not attack the ships bringing across his troops.

Throughout the summer of 1940, German and British pilots fought each other in the 'Battle of Britain' high above southern England. From the start, the odds were stacked against the British:

- The Germans had 824 fighter planes and 1 017 bombers in service. Britain only had about 600 fighter planes.
- It took five minutes for German planes to cross the Channel from France. However, it took 15 minutes for British planes to take off and reach the invading planes after they were spotted.
- Many of the British pilots were part-timers and had not received the same level of training or experience as the Germans who trained 800 new pilots a month. The British trained just 200.

Source D A photograph of RAF pilots 'scrambling' to get to their planes to intercept approaching enemy aircraft. In total, over 3 000 pilots fought against the Germans in the Battle of Britain. Over 2 000 were from Britain but they were joined by New Zealanders (102), Poles (141), Canadians (90), Czechs (86), South Africans (21), Americans (7) and many more.

WORK

1 By July 1940, why were some people calling Hitler the 'Master of Europe'?

2 a What was 'Operation Sealion'? Try to give a really detailed answer.

 b Do you think Hitler had good reason to believe that an invasion of Britain was possible by 15 September? Give reasons for your answer.

Source E The RAF used Spitfire and Hurricane fighter planes whilst the Germans used the Messerschmitt Bf-109. Although the Hurricane was the most commonly used British plane, it was the Spitfire that Germans feared the most.

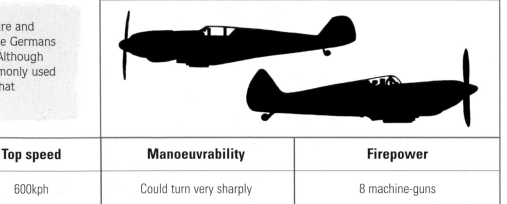

Aeroplane	Top speed	Manoeuvrability	Firepower
Spitfire	600kph	Could turn very sharply	8 machine-guns
Messerschmitt Bf-109	570kph	Could turn quite sharply	2 machine-guns and 2 cannon

Source F A German pilot commenting on each of the main fighter planes. What do you think he means by the phrase, 'could not take as much punishment'?

The Bf-109 was quicker than the Hurricane and about the same as the Spitfire. I think our guns were better too. On the other hand, the British fighters could turn tighter than we could. I also felt that the Bf-109 could not take as much punishment as the British planes.'

Source G A Spitfire pilot who fought in the Battle of Britain (from 'SHP Peace & War', by Shephard, Reid and Shephard, 1993)

'Throughout it all the radio is never silent — shouts, oaths [swearing], encouragements and terse [short, sharp] commands. You single out an opponent. Jockey for position. All clear behind! The bullets from your eight guns go pumping into his belly. He begins to smoke … and you break into a tight turn. Now you have two enemies. The 109 on your tail and your remorseless, ever-present opponent "G", the force of gravity. Over your shoulder you can still see the ugly, questing snout of the 109. You tighten the turn. The Spit protests and shudders and when the blood drains from your eyes you "grey out". But you keep turning, for life itself is at stake. And now your blood feels like molten lead and runs from head to legs. You black out! And you ease the turn to recover in a grey, unreal world of spinning horizons. Cautiously, you climb into the sun … your opponent has gone — disappeared.'

By the end of August, the RAF was only days away from defeat. Its airfields were badly damaged and it didn't have enough pilots. However, the Germans were encountering big problems too. Brand new radar technology meant that the British could detect enemy planes before they reached Britain. A system of 51 radar stations directed British fighters to the Germans in a matter of minutes, leaving them enough fuel to attack the German planes time and time again. In fact, it soon became clear that the Germans were losing more planes than the British. More importantly, the Germans were only making about 150 new planes a month whilst the British were producing over 550!

▲ **Source H** A German bomber, a casualty of the Battle of Britain. Note the British soldier guarding the aircraft from 'souvenir hunters'.

15 September 1940 was a turning point in the Battle of Britain. This was the day that Hitler had singled out as the beginning of the invasion of Britain. But the Luftwaffe had still not defeated the RAF. Hitler did not want to send German troops across the Channel whilst the British still had fighter planes in the air.

At 2:00pm, Prime Minister Winston Churchill asked his air force commander what British fighter planes were available other than the ones in the air. 'There are none', came the reply. However, 15 September saw the final major engagement of the Battle of Britain. On that very day, Germany lost 60 aircraft to Britain's 25! The next day, Hitler postponed Operation Sealion 'until further notice'. He had failed to defeat the RAF by his 15 September deadline and was forced to cancel his invasion plans. Instead, he started to target London in huge night-time bombing raids in an attempt to bomb the British into surrender. This was known as 'the Blitz'.

The RAF pilots who fought in the Battle of Britain became known as the 'Few', after Winston Churchill honoured their victory with this speech: 'Never in the field of human conflict was so much owed by so many to so few'.

▼ **Source I** Fighters and bombers lost by the Luftwaffe in the Battle of Britain. Which set of figures do you think is most accurate and why?

Date	Official British figures	Official German figures	Figures agreed after the war
8–23 Aug	755	213	403
24 Aug–6 Sept	643	243	378
7–30 Sept	846	243	435
TOTAL	**2 244**	**699**	**1 216**

WORK

1 Look at the two fighter planes in **Source E**.
   a Draw the fighter plane you think was most effective.
   b Give reasons for choosing it as the best fighter plane.

2 Look at this list of reasons why Germany lost the Battle of Britain. Explain, in your own words, how each reason made a difference to the outcome of the battle:
   • The British had radar.
   • Hitler lost patience and started bombing London.
   • The Germans miscalculated how many British planes they had shot down.

   Can you add any reasons of your own to explain why Germany lost the Battle of Britain?

3 a In your own words, explain what Churchill meant when he said, 'Never in the field of human conflict was so much owed by so many to so few'.
   b Using **Source A** (page 86) to inspire you, design your own poster to thank the 'Few' and let the British public know how much they owe them.

'Mr and Mrs Jones would like a nice little boy'

AIMS
▶ What was 'evacuation' and why was it necessary?
▶ What was it like to be evacuated?

People in most of the fighting countries expected their cities to be bombed during the war. As soon as war broke out, thousands of children were moved away from the places most likely to be bombed (large industrial cities) and into the countryside where they would be safer. This was known as **evacuation**. The French moved thousands away from their border with Germany. The Germans did the same. In Britain, nearly 1.5 million people had been moved into 'safe zones' by the end of September 1939.

▾ **Source A** Numbers of people evacuated by the British Government in September 1939

The Government took over Britain's entire transport system – all the buses and trains – for four days in order to get people out of the major cities.

Armed with suitcases full of clothes, a gas mask packed into a cardboard box and a name tag tied to their coats, thousands of children left the familiar surroundings of city life for a completely new experience in the countryside. Some would love their new life ... but many others would hate every second of it!

▾ **Source B** An evacuated child, photographed in September 1939

827 000	524 000	13 000	7 000	103 000
School-children	Mothers and children under five	Pregnant women	Blind and disabled people	Teachers

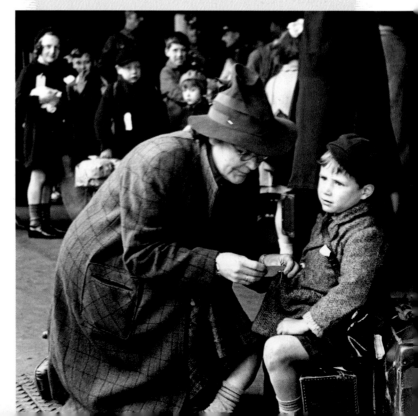

None of the children knew where they were going and nothing prepared them for the ordeal they would go through when they reached their countryside reception areas. There were two main methods of finding a new home or 'foster family'.

Grab a child – the children were lined up and local people would choose the ones they wanted. Obviously, the smarter, cleaner girls would go first ... and the dirtier, scruffy little boys would be left until last.

▼ **Source C** The thoughts of one young girl remembering what happened to her and her brother when she was evacuated (from 'SHP Peace & War', by Shephard, Reid and Shephard, 1993)

'Villagers stood around watching us as we got out of the bus and went into the school. What followed was like an auction. Villagers came in to choose children. "Mr and Mrs Jones would like a nice little boy." Nobody wanted the awkward combination of a girl of 11 and such a small boy, from whom I had promised my mother never to be separated. We were left until the very last. The room was almost empty. I sat on my rucksack and cried.'

Hunt the home – evacuated children, or evacuees as they were called, were led around the town or village and taken door-to-door. Homeowners were asked if they would foster a child for a while.

▼ **Source D** An example of a family who had to hunt for a home (from 'Keep Smiling Through', by Caroline Long, 1989)

'They unloaded us on the corner of the street; we thought it was all arranged, but it wasn't. The billeting officer [the man in charge of housing the children] walked along knocking on doors and asking if they'd take a family. We were the last to be picked. You couldn't blame them; they didn't have any coloured people there in those days.'

PAUSE FOR THOUGHT

Suppose you were evacuated now. You can take just ten of your things with you. Write a list of what you would take, giving reasons for each.

WORK

1 Look at **Source A**.
   a What is meant by the word 'evacuation'?
   b Make a copy of the bar chart, making sure you label it correctly.
   c Look at the different groups of people evacuated in September 1939. Do you think the Government got it right? Which groups of people would you have moved first? Give reasons for each of your choices.

2 Look at **Source B**. By looking at the photograph, write down all you can find out about this boy and what is happening to him.
   • Why do you think he has a label tied to his coat?
   • What is his suitcase for? What do you think it contains?
   • Who do you think the woman is?
   • Why is there a line of children behind him? And why is the boy out of line?
   • How do you think the boy feels? Describe his emotions.

   Compare your answers to the rest of the class.

3 Look at **Sources C** and **D**.
   a Describe the two different methods used to find these two young families a new home.
   b Write down the reasons why they each had problems finding a new home.
   c Do either of the reasons surprise you? Give reasons for your answer.

Evacuation wasn't easy for anyone – evacuees *or* hosts. Some children settled down happily and loved their new lives in their new homes and schools – others hated country life and were homesick. The country people had to put up with a lot too. Some of the children arrived badly clothed, very thin and covered in lice and nits. Some of the 'rougher' evacuees shocked their foster families by swearing and being naughty. One young evacuee in Northallerton, Yorkshire, spent a whole day blocking up the local stream – later that night it was found that he'd flooded six houses and the local church!

▼ **Source E** A 13-year-old boy remembers his evacuation to Buckinghamshire with his sister Rosie

'Rosie whispered. She whispered for days. Everything was so clean. We were given face cloths and toothbrushes. We'd never cleaned our teeth up till then. And hot water came from the tap and there was an indoor toilet. And carpets. And clean sheets. This was all very odd and rather scary.'

▼ **Source F** Unhappy times for an 11-year-old girl evacuated to Cambridgeshire

'My foster mum thought she was onto a good thing with me and the other 11-year-old girl I was put with. We did her shopping for her, cleaned her house, cooked, washed up and even looked after her whining three-year-old when she went out.'

▼ **Source G** An extract from the *Newcastle Evening Chronicle* in 1940. Some boys found country life hard to get used to!

'One evacuated child from the South of England who, on arrival at the billet [his new home], was asked by the hostess, "Would you like some biscuits, dear?" "Biscuits?" the boy replied. "I want some beer and some bloody chips. That's what I get at home!"'

▼ **Source H** One rich woman from Devon, commenting on the evacuees in her house

'I love my six lads from London as if they were my own. They've made this dreary, lonely war quite enjoyable for me.'

FACT: ▶ Picture this

▶ Many city children had never seen a farm animal before. They were shocked to see what cows, chickens and sheep looked like. In October 1939, BBC News broadcast this description of a farm animal written by a young evacuee. Can you guess what animal he's describing?

'It has six sides... at the back it has a tail on which hangs a brush. With this it sends flies away so they don't fall into the milk. The head is for growing horns and so that the mouth can be somewhere... the mouth is to moo with. Under the animal hangs the milk... when people milk, the milk comes and there is never an end to the supply. How the animal does it I have not realised... one can smell it far away. This is the reason for fresh air in the country...'

In case you weren't sure, the boy is describing a cow!

After a few months of life in the British countryside, most children returned to their lives in the city. The enemy bombers hadn't arrived as expected and by March 1940, nearly one million children had gone home. However, later that year the mass bombing of British cities – 'the Blitz' as it was known – began and many children, but not all, returned to the country.

FACT: ▶ Unwanted or forgotten?

▸ When some of the evacuated children finally returned home after the war, they found their homes had been bombed and their parents were missing. Some parents had even abandoned their children on purpose. About 40 000 children remained 'unclaimed' after the war!

▸ **Source I** A Government poster issued in 1940

WISE UP WORD

evacuation

WORK

1 Look at **Source E**. It tells you a lot about the kind of life Rosie led before she was evacuated.
   a Write down at least five things it tells you.
   b How had her life changed?

2 a Who do you think enjoyed evacuation more – the evacuated children or their new families? Try to give reasons for your answer.
   b Did everyone enjoy evacuation? What evidence is there on these pages that some children AND their families did not like evacuation at all?

3 Look at **Source I**.
   a Who is standing next to the tree?
   b What is he doing – and why?
   c Why was this poster produced?
   d What is the message of the poster?

4 Imagine you are one of the children in one of the sources you have been reading. Write a short letter home about your new life. Use your imagination (sensibly) to build up a picture of your new surroundings for your family back home. Compare your letter with other people's letters in your class.

Sir Arthur Harris: war hero or war criminal?

AIMS

▶ Why was Dresden bombed?
▶ Should 'Bomber' Harris be praised or paint bombed?

At about 9:00pm on 13 February 1945, 805 British bomber planes dropped 2 690 tons of bombs on the German city of Dresden. Before long, an area of 11 square miles was burning so ferociously that temperatures reached 1 000 degrees celsius, that's ten times hotter than a boiling kettle! The city blazed for seven days, during which time an estimated 150 000 people were burned to death.

In 1992, a bronze statue of a man in RAF uniform was unveiled in London. The statue was of Sir Arthur 'Bomber' Harris, the Head of Bomber Command and the man whose idea it was to bomb Dresden (see **Source D**). Immediately, protesters threw paint at the statue and demanded its removal.

So do you agree with the protesters – should the statue be removed? Was it wrong to bomb Dresden? Or, as Sir Arthur Harris thought, was the attack necessary to shorten the war and save British lives?

Your task over the next four pages is to formulate an opinion. You must establish:

- Why the attack took place in the first place.
- Why the raid caused so many deaths.
- What the bombing of Dresden achieved.

Your ideas and opinions will then be used to complete a final piece of work.

Why bomb Dresden?

Bomber planes changed the face of war between 1939 and 1945. American and British planes dropped nearly three million tons of bombs on 131 German cities. This killed nearly one million men, women and children, and made eight million people homeless. German planes dropped bombs on British cities too – 40 000 people died in air raids on London, Coventry, Glasgow, Hull and other cities.

When the war began, both sides had tried to use **precision bombing** to hit key targets, such as factories, ports, bridges, major roads and railway stations. The idea was to destroy the enemy's ability to fight by making it impossible to make weapons, build ships or move soldiers around. However, precision bombing didn't work – bombs didn't always hit their targets and damage was often easily repaired – so **area bombing** was introduced instead. This devastating new type of attack meant that whole towns and cities were bombed in order to make sure that *everything* was destroyed ... including the enemies' will to fight!

▼ **Source A** Advice given to the British Government in 1942 by a senior scientific advisor

'Investigations seem to show that having your house destroyed is most damaging to morale ... there seems no doubt that this will break the spirit of the [German] people.'

▼ **Source B** Sir Arthur Harris, Head of RAF Bomber Command, 1942

'Destroy a factory and they rebuild it. If I kill all their workers it takes 21 years to provide new ones.'

In October 1944, a detailed report by the British on Dresden concluded that the city was an 'unattractive target'. In other words, there was no point in bombing the place! However, in January 1945, British spies reported that thousands of German soldiers were collecting in Dresden before being sent off to fight. All of a sudden, Dresden had turned into a key bombing target – and this may have influenced the decision to attack.

▾ **Source C** Sir Arthur Harris, 1945

'Dresden has become the main centre of [the] defence of Germany. It has never been bombed before. And, as a large centre of war industry, it is very important.'

▾ **Source D** A drawing of the statue of Sir Arthur Harris put up in London in 1992. Interestingly, he was the only war commander *not* to have a statue made immediately after the war!

▾ **Source E** A British poster showing Lancaster bombers attacking a target in Germany. What was the purpose of this poster?

The big raids on Germany continue. British war plants share with the R.A.F. credit for these giant operations.

THE ATTACK BEGINS IN THE FACTORY

PAUSE FOR THOUGHT

Before moving onto the next pages, think about the following questions. You may wish to make a few notes.

What is the difference between precision and area bombing?

What evidence is there so far that Dresden was a military target?

What evidence is there so far that Dresden was not a military target?

Why did so many die?

The planes dropped a mixture of **incendiary** and high explosive bombs. Incendiary bombs are specifically designed to start fires. Dresden, being an ancient city with many wooden-framed buildings, started to burn very quickly. The fact that the city was packed with people running away from the Russian army meant that any large fire was sure to kill thousands of people.

The bombs soon created a **firestorm**. In a firestorm, the hot air which rises from burning buildings is replaced by cooler air rushing in from outside. Soon, hurricane-force winds of up to 120mph were 'superheating' the fire.

▼ **Source F** One survivor remembers the firestorm. She was interviewed in 1985.

'I saw people clinging to the railings, burnt to cinders. I kicked what I thought was a big tree stump – but it was a person, burnt to death. There was a big heap of arms, legs, bodies, everything – I tried to piece together a leg, arm, fingers, body – to recognise one of my family – but I passed out.'

▼ **Source G** Victims of the bombing of Dresden, February 1945. Some of the dead have been collected and laid out in this sports hall. Note the survivors arriving to identify bodies of relatives and the coffins stacked up at the back of the hall.

PAUSE FOR THOUGHT

What are incendiary bombs?

Why did Dresden burn so fiercely?

What did the attack achieve?

Historians have argued for years about the bombing of Dresden – did the attack help Britain win the war? Some are sure it helped whilst others questioned whether it was necessary at all. Perhaps the following sources will help you form your opinion.

▼ **Source H** From an article written by historian, Dr Noble Frankland, in 1985

'Every day that the war went on cost the lives of countless more ... so the numbers killed at Dresden, dreadful as they were, were nothing like so dreadful as the numbers of people Hitler was killing... A decisive blow was needed to end the war quickly.'

▼ **Source I** From a letter written by Sir Arthur Harris to Prime Minister, Winston Churchill. Churchill had begun to doubt whether the raid on Dresden was justified.

'Attacks on cities ... tend to shorten the war and so preserve the lives of allied soldiers ... I do not personally regard the whole of the remaining cities of Germany as worth the bones of one British soldier.'

▼ **Source J** Adapted from the report of the British Bombing Survey Unit, set up at the end of the war to study the effects of area bombing on Germany.

'Many German towns were severely devastated by bombing, but the effect on the amount of weapons, tanks and fighter planes the Germans produced was small ... the bombings didn't make the German people lose the will to fight either. The German people proved calmer and more determined than anticipated.'

▼ **Source K** A photograph of Dresden after the bombing. The main railway station and the headquarters of the air force escaped total destruction.

▼ **Source L** The view of an RAF pilot who took part in the attack (from 'Foundation: The Twentieth Century World', by Reynoldson, 1995)

'It struck me at the time, the thought of women and children down there. We seemed to fly for hours over a sheet of fire – a terrific red glow. You can't justify it.'

PAUSE FOR THOUGHT

Look at all the sources written by Sir Arthur Harris (**Sources B, C** and **I**). What is your opinion of Harris based on these sources? Try to use quotes from the sources to back up your statements about him.

What other evidence might a researcher need to collect before forming a fuller opinion of Harris?

▼ **Source M** German war production, 1940–1944

	1940	**1942**	**1944**
Fighter/bomber planes	10 200	14 200	39 500
Tanks	1 600	6 300	19 000
Heavy guns/cannon	4 400	5 100	24 900

! WISE UP WORDS

precision bombing   area bombing
incendiary   firestorm

WORK

You might wish to work in pairs, threes or fours for this task.

A TV company has decided to stage a debate on whether the statue of Sir Arthur Harris should be removed or not. Use the information from these four pages (and anything else you can find out) to produce a report that can be used in the televised debate. Your report must either be in support or against the actions of Harris. Whether your reporting team is for or against Harris, you should try to consider:

- Whether Dresden was an acceptable target or not. Does the use of incendiary rather than explosive bombs tell us anything about the attack?
- Was Harris acting in Britain's best interests to try to win the war – or was he a war criminal guilty of killing innocent people?
- What do you think people felt about the bombing of German cities at the time? Was Harris doing something that most British people supported?
- In a war, is everyone who helps build weapons – including workers and their families – a fair target? Can Harris be criticised for killing any Germans – after all, weren't they all part of Hitler's evil empire?
- Did the bombings actually achieve anything? Did they help Britain win the war?

Why don't you hold the debate in your classroom and present your report as part of the show?

What was Auschwitz like?

> ▸ How did the Nazis organise the mass murder of millions of Jews?
> ▸ What is 'genocide'?

Between 1942 and 1945, at least four million people were sent to Auschwitz, a vast camp just inside German-occupied Poland. It was surrounded by electrified razor-wire fences and tall watchtowers packed with machine-gun carrying guards. Once inside, the 'prisoners' were murdered.

But why was this appalling crime committed? What sort of people were sent to Auschwitz? And what was this death camp really like?

Auschwitz was built as a result of a meeting between leading Nazis, including Hitler, in January 1942. At this time, most of Europe was under German rule and Hitler saw his chance to get rid of all the people he hated – tramps, the mentally impaired, the chronically sick, gypsies, homosexuals, political opponents ... and especially Jews.

For many years, Jewish people had been treated badly all over Germany. But when the war began in 1939, the persecution of the Jews increased rapidly. As the war went on and the Nazis invaded more countries, more Jews became trapped under Hitler's rule. Sometimes they were bricked into separate areas inside cities (called **ghettoes**) or sent to work in camps where they were worked to death.

On 20 January 1942, Nazi leaders decided to carry out what they called 'the final solution' to the Jewish problem. By this, they meant the killing of every Jew in Europe, either by murder or by working them to death. This amounted to an estimated 11 million people ... and Auschwitz was one of six major death or extermination camps specially built for this purpose.

▲ **Source A** The main entrance to Auschwitz. Most people arrived by train, packed into cattle trucks.

▼ **Source B** From the 'Memoirs of Rudolf Hoss', first commandant of Auschwitz

'I was suddenly summoned, Himmler [the man in charge of the "final solution"] said:

The Führer has ordered the Jewish question to be solved once and for all ... I have therefore earmarked [chosen] Auschwitz for this purpose. You will treat this order as absolutely secret, even from your superiors. The Jews are the sworn enemies of the German people and must be eradicated. Every Jew we can lay our hands on is to be destroyed now ... without exception.'

When they arrived at Auschwitz, the prisoners were immediately sorted into two groups: those who looked over 15 years old and were strong and healthy were sent to the left; the old, the sick, pregnant women and women with young children were sent to the right. Those on the left (usually about 10%) were put to work helping to murder the ones on the right. Any refusals would result in an immediate death sentence.

▼ **Source C** The selection process at Auschwitz

▼ **Source D** A map of Europe showing the main concentration and extermination camps. Concentration camps tended to be more like prisons where inmates were put to work in terrible conditions. They were often worked to death. Extermination camps were slightly different – their only purpose was to kill.

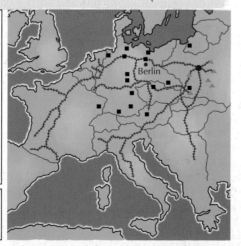

	Number of Jews Killed	%
Poland	3 000 000	90
Germany	210 000	90
Czech	155 000	86
Holland	105 000	75
Hungary	450 000	70
Ukraine	900 000	60
Romania	300 000	50
Russia	107 000	11

▲ Extermination camps
■ Concentration camps
⊢⊣⊢⊣ Transport routes (rail)

WORK

1 Look at **Source B**.

   a What was the 'final solution'?

   b In what way was the final solution different from the way the Nazis treated Jews in the first few years of the war?

2 a What is the difference between a concentration camp and an extermination camp?

   b In your own words, explain what happened to Jewish prisoners as soon as they arrived at Auschwitz.

Those selected to die weren't informed of their fate. To prevent panic, they were told they were going to have a shower and were given soap and towels as they were marched into big chambers disguised as shower rooms. With as many as 2 000 prisoners packed inside at any one time, the doors were sealed and poisonous gas was poured through the vents. In about 30 minutes, everyone was dead. The bodies were later burned.

▼ **Source E** An eyewitness account of a gassing by a Nazi death camp guard, August 1942 (by SS Officer Kurt Gerstein, Belzec, from 'Investigating History', by Neil DeMarco, 2003)

'At last, after 32 minutes, they are all dead... The dead stand like pillars pressed together in the chambers. There is no room to fall or even to lean over. Even in death one can tell which are the families. They are holding hands in death and it is difficult to tear them apart in order to empty the chambers for the next batch. The corpses are thrown out with sweat and urine, smeared with excrement and menstrual blood on their legs. The corpses of children fly through the air. There is no time... Two-dozen dentists open the mouths and look for gold ... some of the workers check genitals and anus for gold, diamonds and valuables.'

▼ **Source F** Another eyewitness account

'The children were taken to an enormous ditch; they were shot or thrown into the fire. No one bothered to see if they were really dead. Sometimes one could hear infants wailing in the fire. If mothers managed to keep their babies with them, a guard took the baby by its legs and smashed it against a wall until only a bloody mess remained in his hands. The mother then had to take this "mess" with her to the "bath" [gas chamber].'

FACT: ▶ Anti-Semitism

▶ **Anti-Semitism**, as hatred of Jewish people is officially known, has been common in Europe for many centuries. Among other things, they have been blamed for the death of Jesus Christ and the outbreak of Black Death in the fourteenth century. At one time or another, they have been driven out of almost every country in Europe and there are few nations today without some record of anti-Semitic violence in their history.

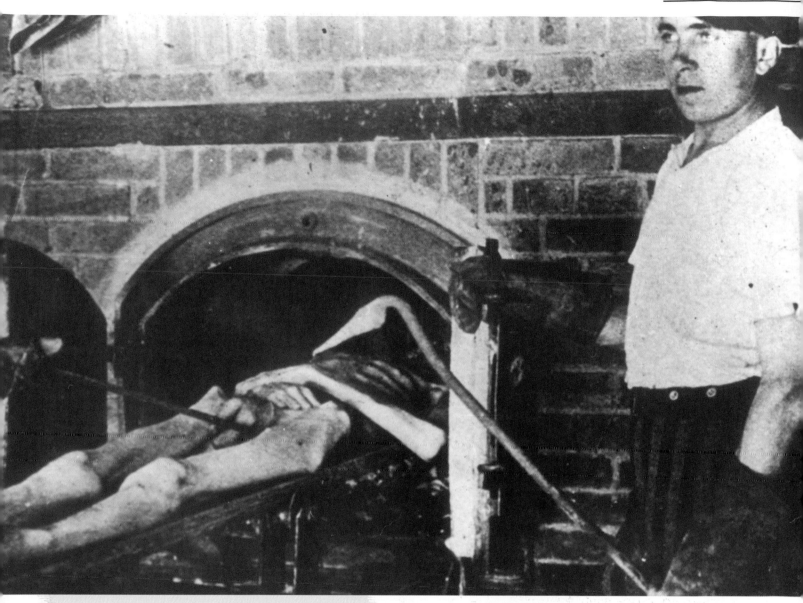

▲ **Source G** A photograph of prisoners' burning corpses

▼ **Source H** Taken from a book published by a Jew, Alex Dekel, who survived his time in Auschwitz. It was common practice for Nazi doctors to experiment with the dried skin of dead victims – it was turned into gloves, shoes, lampshades and even ladies' handbags.

'Major surgery was performed without anaesthetic. Once I witnessed a stomach operation – Mengele [an infamous Nazi death camp doctor who escaped after the war] was removing pieces from the stomach ... it was horrifying.'

WORK

1 a Why did the Nazis tell the Jews they were going for a shower?

  b In your own words, describe what really happened in the 'shower rooms'.

2 Look at **Source E**. The man who witnessed this scene shot himself soon after writing his account.

  a Why do you think he committed suicide?

  b Is there anything in the source that suggests how the man was feeling about what he was witnessing?

3 What does 'anti-Semitism' mean?

4 Is there any evidence on these pages to show that some Nazis did not consider the Jews to be human beings? Back up your thoughts with evidence from the text or sources.

FACT: ▶ The Holocaust

▶ The Nazis' attempt to wipe out the Jewish race is often known as the **Holocaust**. However, many Jews object to this term as it means 'sacrifice'. Some prefer to use the word 'churban', which means 'destruction'.

▼ **Source J** Heinrich Himmler, the man in overall charge of the 'final solution', speaking at a meeting in 1943

'Among ourselves we can talk openly about it, though we will never speak a word in public ... I am speaking about ... the extermination of the Jewish people. That is a page of glory in our history that ... will never be written.'

▼ **Source I** Rows of dead bodies waiting to be buried at a Nazi death camp. It has been estimated that, on average, 4 000 people were murdered *every day* for four years in these camps.

Over six million people, mainly Jews, were killed in death camps like Auschwitz as part of the 'final solution'. When allied soldiers entered these camps after Germany's defeat in 1945, some were so shocked by what they saw that their hair turned white overnight.

At Dachau death camp, American soldiers killed 300 camp guards who had not had time to run away – the surviving inmates killed 200 more! At other camps, soldiers forced the local German population to walk past the unburied bodies, the gas chambers and the ovens to show them what had been going on so close to their homes. Indeed, thousands of people, not only loyal Nazis, helped with the 'final solution' – ordinary people like railway workers, office clerks, policemen and soldiers. 150 German companies used Auschwitz prisoners as slaves –- other firms even competed for the contract to design and build the gas chambers and the ovens in which people were murdered and burned. As reports and photographs of this mass murder started to make its way around the world in newspapers and on news programmes, a new word – **genocide** – entered the vocabulary of a shocked world. It was hoped that genocide – the deliberate extermination of a race of people – would never happen again!

FACT: ▶ Rebellion

▶ There were occasional rebellions in death camps. The most famous of all was in Treblinka in 1943. One of the prisoners managed to get into the weapons store where he handed out guns and grenades. After setting the camp on fire, 150 prisoners managed to escape and 15 guards were killed. However, the Nazis soon regained control and all of the escapees were killed. 550 other prison workers were killed in revenge too!

FACT: ▶ Who knew?

For many years, there has been controversy over how much the allied governments knew about the death camps. Today, most historians agree that the governments of the day knew that something terrible was happening, but not the scale of it. They were in a difficult position too. The camps were deep in the heart of Nazi-occupied Europe and bombing was the only option – but that wasn't a very practical or humane thing to do!

! WISE UP WORDS

genocide   ghettoes   anti-Semitism
Holocaust

HUNGRY FOR MORE?

Rudolf Hess, the man in charge of Auschwitz, escaped from his camp but was captured in 1946. He went on trial with many other leading Nazis later that year. At his trial, he talked about his family and said he didn't like his job. He said he was only following orders. Despite his pleas, he was found guilty of 'war crimes' and sentenced to life imprisonment. As a class, discuss:

• Whether his punishment was fair or not.
• Whether we should continue to hunt Nazi war criminals (some escaped and were never found) and put them on trial, or let the matter drop.

WORK

1 Look at **Source J**.
   a Who was Heinrich Himmler?
   b Why do you think Himmler wanted people to be secretive about the final solution?
   c Do you think Himmler was proud of his work on the final solution? Give a reason for your answer.

2 Suggest reasons why countries didn't do something to stop the suffering at Auschwitz until the war was over.

3 Today, Auschwitz extermination camp is a museum. Many people were against turning it into a museum and wanted it to be pulled down.
   a Why do you think some people wanted Auschwitz destroyed?
   b Do <u>you</u> think we should forget a place like Auschwitz or not? Give reasons for your opinions.

4 a What does the word 'genocide' mean?
   b Find out if genocide has ever happened again.

The end of World War Two: why were nuclear bombs used?

AIMS
▸ How was America pulled into World War Two?
▸ Was it necessary to use nuclear bombs to make Japan surrender?

At 7:55am on Sunday 7 December 1941, 183 Japanese bomber planes launched a surprise attack on Pearl Harbor, an American naval base in the Hawaiian Islands. These islands are part of the USA, despite being thousands of miles away from the rest of the country! In just under two hours, 21 US warships were sunk or damaged, 177 US planes were destroyed and over 2 000 men were killed. The Japanese lost just 29 planes.

The next day, the USA and her major ally, Britain, declared war on Japan. Three days later, Germany and Italy, Japan's official allies, declared war on the USA. Now two more major powers had joined the war – the USA fighting alongside Britain and Japan fighting on Germany and Italy's side.

The USA and Japan had been rivals for many years. Both countries wanted influence and control over the rich lands of the Far East, which contain coal, oil, timber, rubber, gold, gas, copper and so on. By attacking the ships in Pearl Harbor, the Japanese were attempting to make sure that the USA couldn't use their navy to stop them taking all the land they wanted. For a while, their plan seemed to work as the powerful Japanese army, navy and air force took more and more of the Far East (see **Source A**).

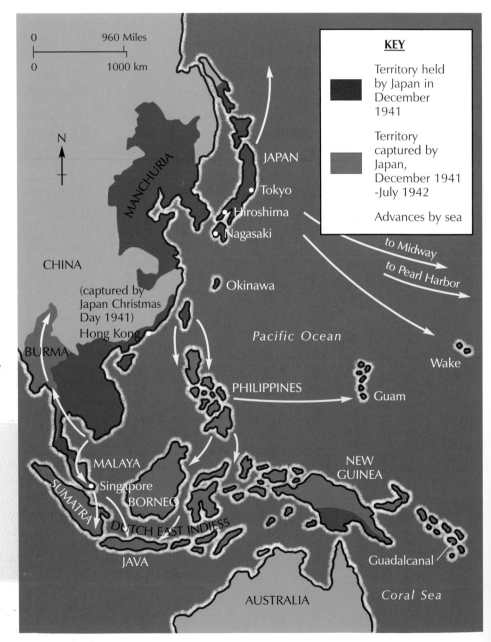

KEY

■ Territory held by Japan in December 1941

Territory captured by Japan, December 1941 –July 1942

Advances by sea

▸ **Source A** The war in the Far East, 1941–1942. By May 1942, the Japanese had gained control of Hong Kong, Guam, Wake, Malaya, Singapore, the Dutch, East Indies, Burma, the Philippines and New Guinea. The loss of Singapore was a huge blow to the British and was Britain's biggest defeat in the war – 80 000 troops were taken prisoner.

By the end of 1942, the USA was fighting back, winning important battles and taking back land in the Far East. By 1944, American soldiers were getting nearer and nearer to Japan, capturing one island at a time. The Japanese had fought fanatically, believing it was a great honour to die for their country. Suicide bombers called **kamikaze** pilots flew planes packed with explosives into American ships, both sides suffering huge losses.

By July 1945, the Japanese were in a desperate position. The war in Europe was over as the Germans and Italians had been beaten. Hitler had poisoned and shot himself on 30 April 1945. Now Japan was fighting on alone and many thought they were close to surrender. The US President, Harry S Truman, had an important decision to make – how was he going to end the war with Japan … quickly?

Final victory

The President decided to use a deadly new weapon – a nuclear bomb, successfully developed in the USA in 1945.

At 8:15am on 6 August 1945, a B29 bomber called Enola Gay dropped the world's first nuclear bomb on the Japanese town of Hiroshima. 80 000 people were killed instantly. Three days later, the Americans dropped another bomb on Nagasaki.

Over 40 000 were killed this time. The next day, Japan gave up and World War Two was over.

But was it right to use it? And why did the USA decide to drop the bombs when many experts believed the Japanese were days away from surrender?

▼ **Source B** A description of some men found hiding in bushes after the bombings (from J Hershey's account of the effects of the bomb, 1946, in 'SHP Peace & War', by Shephard, Reid and Shephard, 1993)

'Their faces were burned, their eye sockets hollow, the fluid from their melted eyes had run down their cheeks. Their mouths were mere swollen, pus-covered wounds, which they couldn't open wide enough to take a drink from a teapot.'

▼ **Source C** A schoolboy remembering the bombings (from BBC's 'Children at War', 1989)

'My uniform was blasted to shreds. The skin at the back of my head, my back, both hands and both legs had peeled off and was hanging down like rags.'

▼ **Source D** This is a photograph of a test explosion of a nuclear bomb on 25 July 1945. (You can see some of the old warships they used to test the blast.) The man who developed the bomb, Robert Oppenheimer, was so overawed by its power, he said, 'I am Death, the destroyer of worlds'. The bomb dropped on Hiroshima was the equivalent of 20 000 tons of dynamite. When US President Truman heard of the bombing, he said, 'This is the greatest thing in history'.

WORK

1 a In your own words, explain what happened at Pearl Harbor on 7 December 1941.

   b Why did the Japanese attack?

2 Write a sentence or two about the word 'kamikaze'.

3 How did the USA achieve final victory in the war against Japan?

So why did the Americans drop the bomb?

Four reasons have been suggested.

The bomb cost a lot of money to develop (over $2 000 million) so the Americans wanted to test it properly.

Some Americans believed that Japan would never surrender. Experts calculated that over half a million American soldiers would die if they had to invade Japan.

The Japanese had been very cruel to any soldiers they had captured. Some Americans felt they needed to be taught a lesson.

The USA wanted to show the world, in particular the USSR, how powerful and advanced they were.

▼ **Source E** A British prisoner of war, 1945 (adapted from 'The Emperor's Guest', by Fletcher-Cooke, 1971)

'There is no doubt in my mind that these bombs saved many more lives than the tens of thousands they killed. They saved prisoners of war ... allied servicemen and millions of Japanese – for, let there be no mistake, if the [Japanese] Emperor and his cabinet had decided to fight on, the Japanese would, literally, have fought to the last man.'

FACT: ▶ Hot stuff!

▶ The temperature at the centre of the explosion reached 300 000 centigrade, fifty times hotter than the surface of the sun. Some people were vaporised, others died days, weeks, months or years later from horrific burns or radiation sickness.

A photograph of the city of Hiroshima after the bomb. In total, 70 000 of the city's 78 000 buildings were totally destroyed.

▼ **Source F** From a 1965 interview with James Byrnes, US Secretary of State

'We were talking about the people who hadn't hesitated at Pearl Harbor to make a sneak attack, destroying not only ships but the lives of many American sailors.'

▼ **Source G** This is what Kasai Yukiko, a high school pupil, was told to do by her teacher if the Americans invaded in 1945

'Even killing one American soldier will do. Use your awls [woodwork tools] for self defence. Aim for the enemy's belly. Understand? The belly? If you don't kill at least one, you don't deserve to live.'

▼ **Source H** A British cartoon from 1945

JAPAN WAS SEEKING PEACE <u>BEFORE</u> THE FIRST ATOM BOMB WAS DROPPED ON HIROSHIMA, ACCORDING TO DOCUMENTS JUST LEAKED TO THE U.S. PRESS.

"DON'T YOU SEE, THEY <u>HAD</u> TO FIND OUT IF IT WORKED ..."

▼ **Source I** Admiral William Leahy, one of President Truman's advisors in 1945. He wrote this in 1950.

'This barbarous weapon was of no real use in our war against Japan. They were already defeated and were ready to surrender ... the scientists and others wanted to make this test because of the vast sums that had been spent.'

▼ **Source J** From a booklet against nuclear weapons, published in 1985

'There were two slightly different types of bomb. The second bomb was dropped to see if it worked as well as the first.'

▼ **Source K** Some comments made in interviews by people who lived in Hiroshima in 1995. They are in answer to the question: 'Why do you think the bombs were dropped?'

'Mainly to show the military strength of the USA at that time.'

'To damage Japan and demonstrate the power of the allied countries.'

'Because Hiroshima was a big city which was worth destroying. There was a military base there.'

'Because they had them.'

'This is not a simple issue; there are many reasons. They were: to stop the war, to save American soldiers and to show their power.'

'To experiment with their new technology but couldn't they have dropped it on an uninhabited island nearby?'

(!) WISE UP WORD

kamikaze

WORK

1 a Copy out the list of four different reasons (page 106) that have been suggested to explain why the USA dropped nuclear bombs on Japan in 1945.
  b Look through **Sources E** to **K**. All the sources can be matched to one of the reasons. Try to match each of the seven sources (**E, F, G, H, I, J, K**) to a reason from your list. Write out the evidence from the source that made you match it to one of the four reasons.

2 Do you think the USA was right to use nuclear weapons? This is a very difficult question to answer so think about it carefully and weigh up all the evidence over the last four pages. Remember, there are good arguments on both sides.

United Nations?

AIMS
▶ How does the United Nations work?
▶ What was the 'Cold War' and why did it start?

Towards the end of World War Two, Britain, Russia and the USA realised that something must be done to prevent such a terrible war ever happening again. After a series of meetings, the leaders of the three countries decided to set up a club of nations and invited all other countries of the world to join (except Germany and Japan). A special skyscraper was planned in New York to house the representatives of each country where, it was hoped, problems between nations could be settled through discussion and not fighting. This new organisation had a name – the United Nations Organisation, or UN for short – and it held its first meeting in April 1945, a few weeks before World War Two officially ended. Representatives from 51 countries were there.

Security Council

Five of the most powerful countries were members of the Security Council (Britain, France, USA, Russia and China). Six other countries (later ten) sent representatives to sit on the Council for two years at a time. They still meet whenever there is a dispute between any countries that looks like boiling over into war. They can stop one country attacking another by:
- asking them to stop
- asking all other members of the UN to stop trading with the quarrelling states until a shortage of supplies forces them to give up the war
- sending in soldiers – or peacekeepers – from several UN countries to stop the fighting or prevent it from spreading

Any decisions need a 'yes' from all five permanent members.

The General Assembly

A sort of world parliament, with each country having one vote.

Secretary-General

A key person who manages the whole operation and leads the UN.

World Health Organisation (WHO) (see **Source C**)

Mounts health campaigns, does research, runs clinics and vaccinates against infectious diseases.

▼ **Source A** The United Nations Building in New York. It was opened in 1952.

▼ **Source B** The UN has a **charter** or collection of aims, which was first listed in September 1945. All countries must sign the UN Declaration of Human Rights before being allowed to join.

UN DECLARATION OF HUMAN RIGHTS

- All human beings are born free and equal.
- Everyone has the right to life, liberty and freedom from fear and violence.
- Everyone has the right to protection of the law without discrimination.
- Everyone has the right to a fair trial and will not be arrested without good reason.
- No one shall be a slave.
- No one shall be tortured or punished in a cruel, inhumane or degrading way.
- Everyone has the right to seek **asylum** from persecution in other countries.
- Adult men and women have the right to marry, regardless of their race or religion.

International Labour Organisation (ILO)

Tries to protect workers all over the world by improving their conditions, pay, rights and insurance.

Children's Fund (UNICEF)

Helps underfed, poorly treated or neglected children throughout the world.

International Court of Justice

Based in Holland. Fifteen judges, each from a different nation, settle legal disputes between countries before they lead to war.

Educational, Scientific and Cultural Organisation (UNESCO)

Tries to get countries to share each other's films, books, music, sport and scientific discoveries so that they understand each other more and are less likely to fight.

▼ **Source C** One of the WHO's greatest successes was the elimination of smallpox, one of history's biggest killers, through a massive vaccination programme.

▶ **Source D** The UN logo. What do you think it means? By 1960, 100 countries were members of the UN. This increased to 127 members by 1970, 154 by 1980 and 184 by 2000.

WORK

1   Imagine you are representing your country at one of the first meetings of the UNO. You are holding a press conference. What would be your answers to these questions?

- Why is this new organisation necessary?
- What is the Security Council and how can it stop one country attacking another?
- Are all nations of the world in the UNO?
- Why do all countries have to sign the Declaration of Human Rights before being allowed to join the UN?
- People throughout the world are weak and vulnerable after the war – how will the UNO help them?

2   Look at **Source B**. Do you think that some of the rights are more important than others? Explain your answer carefully.

3   Look at **Source D**.

   a   Draw the logo of the UN.

   b   Explain what you think the logo means.

Look at this fantastic photograph carefully (**Source E**). It was taken at a meeting of the United Nations Security Council in 1953. It shows the USSR's Andrei Vishinski shouting at USA's representative, Henry Cabot Lodge. Britain's Sir Gladwyn Jebb is sitting in the middle with his head in his hands!

The USA and the USSR had fought together as allies to defeat Nazi Germany in World War Two. They had both joined the United Nations, determined to prevent future wars. So why had these two former allies fallen out in such a big way?

When World War Two ended, the USA and the USSR were the most powerful countries in the world ... by a long way. They had more soldiers, tanks, submarines and planes than any other country – and because they each had a population of over 200 million, it was little wonder that these two countries were soon known as the **superpowers**!

Millions of men, women and children were killed during the war but the USSR suffered more than most – at least 20 million were killed in four years of fighting. As you might expect, the USSR never wanted to be invaded again. Their solution was to grab as much land as possible and turn the countries in between the USSR and Germany into a buffer zone or safety area. The Russians claimed they were taking this land to make themselves feel safer, not because they were greedy for more land.

▲ **Source E** A 1953 UNO meeting

▶ **Source F** The division of Europe after 1945. When the Germans surrendered on 7 May 1945, Germany was immediately divided into four zones. In 1949, the USA, Britain and France allowed their three zones to join together and form West Germany, a new democratic nation. The USSR insisted that the Eastern part of Germany became a Communist state. The country remained divided until 1989. 'Iron Curtain' was the nickname Winston Churchill used to describe the imaginary dividing line between Capitalist and Communist countries.

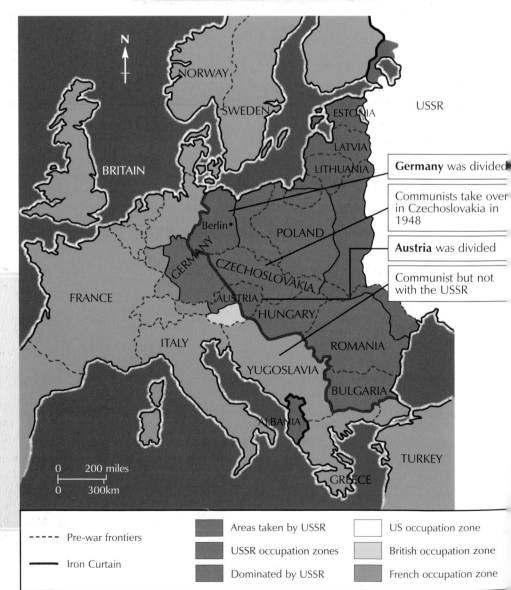

Germany was divided

Communists take over in Czechoslovakia in 1948

Austria was divided

Communist but not with the USSR

----- Pre-war frontiers	Areas taken by USSR	US occupation zone
	USSR occupation zones	British occupation zone
—— Iron Curtain	Dominated by USSR	French occupation zone

Despite what the Russians said about their buffer zone, the USA and her allies (Britain and France, for example) were concerned and suspicious about the growing threat of the USSR. Whenever the Russians took over a new country, they insisted that the government should be a Communist one. Communism meant that all farms, factories and so on were to be owned by the workers and run by the government to make a profit for everyone. This sounded fine, but in reality, the Russian leader, Stalin, was a cruel dictator who ran his new Communist empire very harshly and allowed no criticism. Was he trying to spread his Communist way of life to all the other countries in Europe, possibly the world?

The USA and the rest of Western Europe ran their countries very differently. They believed in Capitalism – farms, factories and companies were owned by individuals who ran them to make a profit (capital) for themselves. Also, all governments were elected by the people ... who could criticise the government if they wanted to.

Communism and Capitalism, therefore, were directly opposite to each other. By 1950, the world had once again divided itself into two armed camps – the Capitalist democracies like the USA, Britain and France on one side and the Communist countries, dominated by the USSR (the 'mother country') on the other. Each side began to build weapons on a massive scale – and now each side had nuclear bombs too.

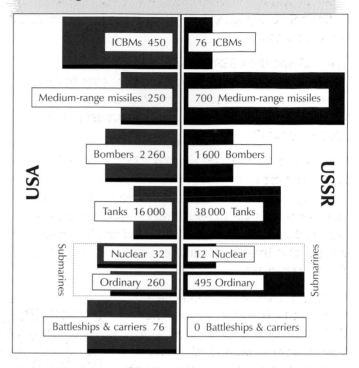

▼ **Source G** The weapons race between the USA and the USSR, 1963. ICBMs are Inter-Continental Ballistic Missiles – nuclear rockets capable of travelling thousands of miles.

USA		USSR
ICBMs 450		76 ICBMs
Medium-range missiles 250		700 Medium-range missiles
Bombers 2 260		1 600 Bombers
Tanks 16 000		38 000 Tanks
Nuclear 32 (Submarines)		12 Nuclear (Submarines)
Ordinary 260		495 Ordinary
Battleships & carriers 76		0 Battleships & carriers

Relations between the Capitalists in the Western part of the world and the Communists in the East got so bad that some people thought that a new war had started. Not a traditional war with actual fighting, but a 'cold war' – a war of words, propaganda and threats. This situation remained the same for the next 45 years.

WORK

1 a Which countries were the world's first modern 'superpowers'?

   b Why do you think they got this nickname?

2 Look at **Source F**.

   a Why, according to the Russians, did they take lots of land after the war?

   b Look for the 'Iron Curtain', a red dividing line on the map. What was the difference between the countries on the east and west of the 'Iron Curtain'?

   c The 'Iron Curtain' wasn't a real curtain! Why do you think Winston Churchill described the border between eastern and western Europe as one?

3 Copy out and complete the following paragraph, choosing the correct word from the bracket each time.

   By (1950/1960), the world had been divided into (three/two) armed camps. The (USSR/USA) dominated one side, the (USA/Japan) the other. The USSR was a (continent/Communist) country where everything was owned by the (workers/children) but run by the government. The USA was a (Capitalist/capsized) country where everything was owned and run by (many different/no) people. (Everyone/No one) could vote so it was a (democracy/delicacy).

4 a In your own words, explain what is meant by the term 'cold war'.

   b Why do you think the USA and USSR developed so many weapons?

The Cold War lasted for 45 years. Sometimes the USA and the USSR got on quite well; at other times they came close to war ... very close!

The closest the two enemies ever came to a full-scale war was in October 1962. For 13 days, the world faced the very real possibility of World War Three. So why did this terrible situation occur? Exactly how close was a nuclear attack? And how did this crisis – and the Cold War itself – finally come to an end?

The USA and the USSR went to the brink of nuclear war over Cuba, a Caribbean island 90 miles from the American coast. In 1959, a young Communist called Fidel Castro had seized control of Cuba. The USA, fearing a Communist country so close to their own, ordered a top secret invasion of Cuba. The invasion was a total flop and a great embarrassment for the US President, John F Kennedy. Castro, fearing another invasion, asked the new Russian leader, Khrushchev, if he wished to set up any missile bases in Cuba. The Russians gladly accepted.

On 14 October 1962, a US spy plane discovered nuclear missile bases, which were now in easy range of most major American cities – New York, Washington, Boston, Miami and Chicago.

▼ **Source I** A photograph of a missile base in Cuba, taken by a US spy plane

▼ **Source H** A map showing American cities in range of a Russian nuclear missile attack from Cuba

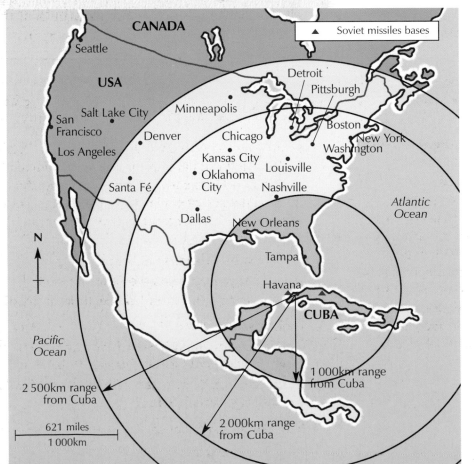

US spy planes spotted more missiles on their way from the USSR to Cuba and the USA sent warships to stop the missiles reaching their destination. As the world held its breath, the two leaders – Kennedy and Khrushchev – negotiated with each other. Finally, on 27 October, an agreement was reached. The Americans promised not to invade Cuba and agreed to remove some of their own missile bases near Russia – and the Russians agreed to turn their ships around. The world breathed a huge sigh of relief when the news was announced – this was the closest the world has ever come to World War Three!

▲ **Source J** A photograph of a Russian ship, on its way to Cuba. Can you guess (or see) what it is carrying?

▼ **Source K** Robert McNamara, one of President Kennedy's advisors, speaking in March 1988

'It was a beautiful fall [autumn] evening, the height of the crisis, and I went up into the open air to look and to smell it, because I thought it was the last Saturday I would ever see.'

▼ **Source L** Fyodor Burlatsky, one of Khrushchev's advisors

'I phoned my wife and told her to drop everything and to get out of Moscow. I thought the bombers were on the way.'

Surprisingly, the Cuban missile crisis led to an improvement in relations between the USA and the USSR. Both countries had come so close to nuclear war, they realised that if things were to get so bad again, the end result might not be so peaceful. In 1963, both countries agreed to stop testing new nuclear bombs and a direct telephone line – the 'Hot Line' – was set up so they could negotiate more easily in future. Despite other situations, where America or America's ally fought the USSR's ally, never once did an American soldier fight a Russian during the whole of the Cold War.

The Cold War began to thaw in the 1980s. By then, many of the countries that the USSR had taken over at the end of World War Two were demanding, and getting, their independence. The Russian leader, Mikhail Gorbachev, was willing to give these people what they wanted. By the end of 1991, even Gorbachev himself was out of power and Communism was finished. The United States, which stood for democracy and Capitalism, had 'won' the Cold War.

! WISE UP WORDS

asylum   charter   superpowers   Cold War

WORK

1 a Imagine you work for the US President in October 1962 and you have just been handed **Sources H, I** and **J**. In 15 minutes you are due to meet the President and brief him about the sources. For each source, write a sentence or two explaining:
   • what it shows;
   • how serious you think it is;
   • what you think you should do about it.
   b How was a third world war eventually avoided?

2 Look at **Sources K** and **L**.
   a According to the writers of these sources, how close was a third world war in October 1962?
   b Can we trust these sources? Think carefully and give reasons for your answer.

3 How did the Cold War end?

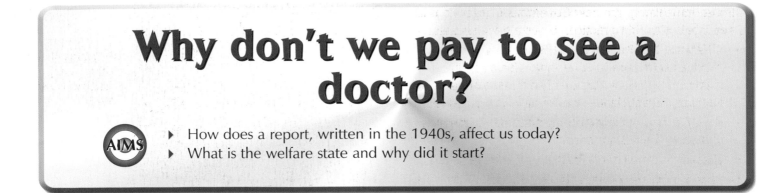

Why don't we pay to see a doctor?

AIMS
▸ How does a report, written in the 1940s, affect us today?
▸ What is the welfare state and why did it start?

There is almost no one in Britain who isn't helped at some time or another by what is known as the **welfare state**. This is the name of the system by which the Government aims to help those in need, mainly the old, the sick and the unemployed. It is sometimes called **social security**. It aims to make sure that nobody goes without food, shelter, clothing, medical care, education or any other basic need because they can't afford it.

WELFARE STATE

FOR CHILDREN
- CLINICS
- CHEAP - OR FREE - MILK AND FOODS
- CHEAP - OR FREE - SCHOOL DINNERS
- EDUCATION
- FREE DENTAL CARE AND SPECTACLES

FOR ADULTS AND THEIR FAMILIES
- FREE DOCTORS
- FREE HOSPITALS
- CHEAP MEDICINE
- FAMILY ALLOWANCES
- SICK PAY
- UNEMPLOYMENT PAY OR DOLE
- TRAINING
- PENSIONS FOR THOSE UNABLE TO WORK
- MONEY FOR THOSE ON NO INCOME OR ONLY VERY SMALL INCOMES
- MATERNITY GRANTS

FOR OLD PEOPLE
- RETIREMENT PENSIONS
- SPECIAL HOMES
- HOME HELP
- MEALS AT HOME
- FINANCIAL HELP WITH FUNERAL COSTS

Study **Source A** carefully. It gives a basic outline of the welfare state. You and your family will almost certainly have been helped out by this system at one time or another.

Although we take the things outlined in **Source A** for granted today, it is not a system that has been in place for many years. From 1906, the Government had introduced *some* help for the most vulnerable sections of society – free school meals for poorer children, free school medical check-ups and treatment, small old-age pensions for the over 70s and basic sick and 'dole' pay – but nothing on the same scale as what was introduced after World War Two.

Towards the end of the war, a man named Sir William Beveridge wrote a report about the state of Britain. It outlined some of the problems that Britain would have to face once the war was over and suggested ways to improve things. In a Britain where people hoped that life would be better once the war was over, it became a surprise best-seller.

As the war ended, an election was held to decide who would run the country after the war. The Labour Party promised to follow Beveridge's advice but the Conservative Party, led by Winston Churchill, refused to make such a promise. The Labour Party won the election easily – and Winston Churchill, the man who had led Britain during the war, was out of power!

▲ **Source A** When this system was first designed, it was hoped that it would provide 'security from the cradle to the grave'. What do you think this means?

Almost immediately, the new Government began to put Beveridge's plan into practice. It was a huge success:

- A National Health Service (NHS) was set up to provide health care for everyone. This made all medical treatment – doctors, hospitals, ambulances, dentists and opticians – free to all who wanted it.
- A weekly family allowance payment was introduced to help with childcare costs.
- The very poor received financial help or 'benefits'.
- Pensions for the elderly and disabled were increased.
- The school leaving age was raised to 15 to give children a greater chance of a decent education and more free university places were created.
- Twelve new towns were created. By 1948, 280 000 council homes were being built each year.

Of course, all this cost money. All workers would have to pay for the service through taxes and **National Insurance** contributions. This is how the welfare state is paid for today … and EVERYONE pays National Insurance when they get a job (including you!).

Despite the huge cost of the welfare state, it still remains a remarkable achievement. It didn't stay totally free for long – working people today have to pay for prescriptions, dental treatment and other things – but, on the whole, the welfare state ensures that no one is deprived of food, shelter, clothing, medical care, education or any other essentials because they can't afford them.

◀ **Source C** A Labour Party election poster, 1945

> ▼ **Source B** Frederick Rebman, speaking in 2004, remembering the introduction of the welfare state

'We were sorry to see Churchill voted out, he was our war leader, but he never promised to give the new ideas a go. The Labour Party did you see, and they publicised this in all the papers … servicemen [men in the army, navy and air force] like me expected so much after the war, perhaps Utopia [a perfect world], and the welfare state seemed to be a good start. I didn't mind the idea of paying a bit more of my salary to know that a doctor or a dentist was there if I needed them. I felt it was worth it, that the Government cared about us a bit more I suppose … I think there was a bit of a rush when the NHS first started. There were stories of people going and getting whole new sets of teeth, new glasses, even wigs. Perhaps they'd have struggled on before with their short-sightedness or their painful teeth, but now they didn't have to.'

! WISE UP WORDS

welfare state   National Insurance
social security

WORK

1 Copy and complete this paragraph.

Sir William _____ wrote his report about the state of _____ shortly before the end of the _____. He suggested that the Government should provide a national _____ service and provide social _____ 'from the _____ to the _____'. In the general election of _____, the _____ Party was elected and decided to try out his ideas.

2 a In your own words, explain what the term 'welfare state' means.

   b Draw your own version of **Source A**, showing the different benefits a person may receive at different stages in their life. Call your diagram, 'From the cradle to the grave'.

3 Look at **Source B**.

   a According to the source, why did the Labour Party win the election in 1945?

   b Why do you think people rushed out to get 'whole new sets of teeth, new glasses, even wigs' when the NHS first started?

HISTORY MYSTERY

Man on the moon ... or was he?

During the 1950s and 1960s, the USA and the USSR were competing in a frantic 'space race' to be the first to conquer space and put a man on the moon. Both sides were determined to prove that *their* country and way of life were superior.

American pride was dented in April 1961 by the news that Yuri Gagarin, a Russian astronaut, had become the first human to orbit the earth. It seemed that Russia had won the space race ... but not for long! The US President, John F Kennedy, responded by setting what many thought was an impossible target: 'To land a man on the moon and return him safely to earth ... by 1970!' Just eight years later, on 20 July 1969, America's *Apollo 11* moon-mission triumphed and Neil Armstrong became the first man to walk on the surface of another world. Millions across earth watched the event 'live' on their TV sets. To many Americans, and other countries of the world, landing a man on the moon was more of an achievement than putting one in space – it showed the greatness of the American way of life and its superiority over the Russians.

▼ **Evidence A** An artist's impression of the front page of the *Daily Mail* newspaper, which celebrates the news

Daily ★ Mail

MONDAY, JULY 21, 1969

At last moment Armstrong grabs the controls to hop over 'football-field crater'

MAN ON THE MOON

From ANGUS MACPHRSON, Houston, Sunday

They're on the Moon! While the world held its breath Neil Armstrong and Edwin Aldrin touched down today dead on time in their landing craft Eagle and began preparing for man's first fantastic steps on another planet.

As they touched down at 9.17 and 40 sec. BST tonight Armstrong revealed a last moment hitch that might have meant disaster.

He had to take control of the Eagle landing craft back from the computer at the very last stage. 'The auto-targeting was taking us right into a football -

▼ **Evidence B** Buzz Aldrin

'That's one small step for a man, one giant leap for mankind!'.

These were the famous words that Neil Armstrong was meant to say as he put his feet on the moon's surface on 20 July 1969. However, he got his lines wrong and forgot the 'a' in the heat of the moment!

This is a picture of Buzz Aldrin, the second man on the moon – why do you think there are no pictures of Armstrong's historic steps? The two men stayed on the moon for nearly one whole earth day.

But as news of the moon landing spread across the earth, another famous story was just beginning. As photographs and film were released, some people began to say the whole mission, including the moon landing itself, were faked. They said that in 1969, Americans didn't have the technology to land men on the moon (and get them back safely) and started to pick apart each and every part of the mission. Even the photograph on this page came under scrutiny (**Evidence C**). Some wondered why the photograph was of such good quality. And where are the stars – aren't they meant to be in the background?

Controversy still rages over this historic event today. Did the Americans fake the landings just to 'get one over' on the Russians? Was it faked in 1969 because the President had promised the American public to put a man on the moon before 1970? Were the moon landings filmed in a TV studio rather than on the moon itself? These pages will ask you to form your opinions on this great debate – was man on the moon in July 1969 … or not?

▼ **Evidence C** To those who think the landings were faked, this picture is often used to back up their arguments. They say the photograph is <u>too</u> perfect – it looks like the astronaut posed for it.

- The cameras were mounted on the front of each astronaut's space units (with no auto focus). So why is it such a good picture? Did professional photographers take them in a special studio?

- Why is the flag fluttering? There's no atmosphere on the moon, no breeze at all. A flag wouldn't wave in a vacuum so there must have been a slight wind on the film set.

- Why do the footprints look like they've been set in wet sand? There is no water on the moon to make this happen, so surely the footprints should have disappeared like the dry sand on a beach.

- And where are the stars? The sky should be full of them!

In 2001, a survey in America showed that 30% of US citizens believed the 1969 moon landings were faked. It clearly remains a very 'hot topic', not just in America, but all over the world. Study these photographs, facts and written sources very carefully. These cover the most controversial areas of the whole topic.

▼ **Evidence D** A photograph of a moon rock. Can you see the letter 'C'? The people who think the landings were faked use this photograph to back up their theory that the whole thing was filmed in a TV studio. They suggest that every rock on the 'faked' moon surface was individually labelled, starting at 'A'. This is a close-up photo of rock 'C' (which the people who built the set forgot to turn over!).

▼ **Evidence E** From a science website

'Pictures from astronauts transmitted from the moon don't include stars in the dark lunar sky – an obvious production error! What happened? Did NASA [the US government agency responsible for space travel] film-makers forget to turn on the lights? Most photographers already know the answer: It's difficult to capture something very bright and something else very dim on the same piece of film … astronauts striding across the bright lunar soil in their sunlit spacesuits were dazzling. Setting a camera up properly for a glaring space unit could make the background stars too faint to see.'

▼ **Evidence F** From a website that tries to prove that the moon landings were <u>not</u> faked (www.redzero.demon.co.uk)

'[The mark on the rock] is not a 'C'. The photograph is a copy of the original photograph. If you look at the original, taken in 1969, the 'C' disappears. This is simply because all it is, is a tiny hair that has got into one of the copies along the way.'

▼ **Evidence G** Further evidence that the moon landings were not faked

'THE ASTRONAUTS RECEIVED A GREAT DEAL OF TRAINING BEFORE THEY LEFT EARTH; PART OF THIS WAS IN THE OPERATION OF CAMERAS, WHICH WERE SPECIALLY DESIGNED TO BE USED BY THE ASTRONAUTS WITH THEIR SUITS ON. THE *APOLLO* ASTRONAUTS TOOK AROUND 17 000 PHOTOGRAPHS … AND THERE'S PLENTY OF NOT-SO-GREAT ONES THAT NASA HAVE NEVER PUBLISHED … ONLY THE BEST ONES WERE RELEASED TO THE WORLD.'

▶ Evidence H The *Apollo 11* sleeve patch, worn by the astronauts on the mission. The eagle is one of the symbols of the USA, whilst the olive branch is a sign of peace.

▼ Evidence I From a space website (www.badastronomy.com)

'THE FLAG ISN'T WAVING. IT LOOKS LIKE THAT BECAUSE OF THE WAY IT'S BEEN PUT UP. THE FLAG HANGS FROM A HORIZONTAL ROD, WHICH PULLS OUT FROM THE VERTICAL ONE. IN *APOLLO 11*, THEY COULDN'T GET THE ROD TO EXTEND COMPLETELY, SO THE FLAG DIDN'T GET STRETCHED FULLY. IT HAS A RIPPLE IN IT LIKE A CURTAIN THAT IS NOT FULLY CLOSED … IT APPEARS TO HAVE FOOLED A LOT OF PEOPLE INTO THINKING IT WAVED.'

▼ Evidence J CNN News, 10 September 2002

'Beverly Hills, California, USA – detectives are investigating a complaint that retired astronaut Buzz Aldrin punched a man in the face after being asked to swear on a Bible that he had been to the moon … [the man] said he does not believe Aldrin or anyone else has ever walked on the moon.'

PAUSE FOR THOUGHT

Can we ever be really sure that man landed on the moon? How can we find out for sure? Think carefully before giving an answer.

WORK

Now you've had a chance to look through the evidence, it's time to decide whether YOU think the USA put man on the moon in 1969.

Step 1 Find reasons why the USA felt it was really important to put a man on the moon before the USSR.

What was the 'space race'? How had the USSR dented American pride in 1961? What had President Kennedy promised and why? Why would the USA *want* to beat the Russians and put a man on the moon before them?

Step 2 Find evidence that the moon landings were faked.

Think about the photographs. What is 'wrong' with some of them? Make notes on the suspicions surrounding the moon landings.

Step 3 Find any evidence that the moon landings were <u>not</u> faked.

Can any of the 'errors' on the photographs be explained? Make notes that answer some of the suspicions about the landings from **Step 2**.

Finally Time to make up your mind!

Were the moon landings faked? Write a short report for a children's TV programme about the moon landings. In your report, you should express your opinion about the moon landing debate. Remember, you must back up your theory with evidence.

Whatever happened to the British Empire?

▶ What factors caused the decline of the world's largest ever Empire?

▶ How did India gain its independence from British rule?

In 1901, Queen Victoria died. At the time, Britain ruled about 450 million people living in 56 different places – or colonies – all over the world. Put simply, the British Empire was the biggest empire the world had ever known.

Fifty years later, after two world wars, the British Empire was breaking apart. More and more countries in the Empire wanted nothing to do with Britain. They wanted their chance to run their countries themselves – they wanted their independence. And Britain, still trying to rebuild after World War Two, was in no position to stop them. One by one, nearly all Britain's colonies became independent countries (today, Britain's Empire consists of only a few tiny islands). These next six pages focus on one of these former colonies, India, and its struggle for freedom from British rule up to 1947.

India was one of Britain's largest possessions. It was the colony that many Britons treasured most, calling it the 'Jewel in the Crown' of the Empire. Even Queen Victoria herself enjoyed the title 'Queen of Great Britain and Empress of India'. One of the reasons for this pride was their record of achievement. The British took much of the latest technology to India in an attempt to transform the landscape and 'civilise' the Indian population.

FACT: ▶ British help?

▶ By 1900, the British had built nearly 50 000 miles of railway through India. They built dams to help flood areas and dug nearly 70 000 miles of canal. They also introduced a new legal system and helped to settle ancient feuds between rival areas and regions ... whether the Indians wanted these things or not!

▶ **Source A** The views of Lord Curzon, a former viceroy of India. Two-thirds of India were ruled by the viceroy. He was the king or queen's representative in India – basically, he ruled it for them! The other third of India was governed by Indian princes ... who had to have British advisors to help them (and make sure they were doing what the British wanted). Thousands of British soldiers were stationed in India too.

▼ **Source B** British India factfile. The present day countries of India, Pakistan, Burma, Bangladesh and Sri Lanka were all included within the borders of British India.

Size
Larger than the continent of Europe
Fifteen times bigger than the British Isles

Population and religion
300 million, 1/5 of the population of the world
207 million Hindus
62.5 million Muslims
6 million Sikhs
Plus millions of Buddhists, Christians and others

Languages
15 main languages – Hindu and Pakistani – northern and central areas
Urdu and Gujarati – west
Bengali – east
Tamil – south

Main resources
Cotton
Tea
Iron ore
Coal
Rice
Diamonds

'Wherever the British go ... we replace misery, poverty, cruelty and disorder with peace, justice, wealth, humanity and freedom.'

► **Source C** A painting of 'Lord Curzon's Durbar', held when King Edward VII became King after Queen Victoria's death. A durbar was a large ceremonial meeting and this one was so big that they had to build a railway track five miles long to take people around it. All of the most important people in India attended. It went on for ten days and finished with a Christian church service. The elephants pictured here carry Indian princes and are decorated with fine cloth, gold, silver, diamonds and pearls valued at £100 000 *each* in today's money!

WORK

1 This word search contains seven words or names connected with British India. When you find each one, write a sentence about it in your book.

M	U	S	L	I	M	P
L	S	R	O	T	N	Q
V	I	C	E	R	O	Y
S	K	O	F	E	Z	H
T	H	T	N	M	R	I
E	E	T	P	Z	U	N
A	O	O	Q	R	C	D
P	L	N	N	M	I	U

2 a What advantages did the British think they introduced to India?

  b What do you think some Indians thought about British rule in India?

3 Look at **Source C**. In your own words, explain what is going on in the picture.

By 1900, many educated Indians started to believe that India should be free from British control. A political group called the Indian National Congress was formed to bring this about, but despite holding meetings and organising demonstrations, the British ignored their demands.

In 1914, Indians fought alongside British soldiers in the Great War (see **Source D**). India itself gave Britain a huge amount of money, food and materials – and nearly 50 000 Indian soldiers died in the trenches!

▼ **Source D** More than 800 000 Indian soldiers fought on the British side in the Great War. This photograph was taken in 1914 and shows Earl Kitchener (the man on the poster on page 26) inspecting troops from India.

In 1919, the British Government responded to Indian demands for a greater say in running their country and made slight changes to the way India was governed. Law-making councils were set up in each province and over five million wealthy Indians were given the vote. However, the British Government, based in London, still controlled taxation, the police, the law courts, the armed forces, education and much more. Whilst some welcomed the changes as a step in the right direction, others were bitterly disappointed. A demonstration in the town of Amritsar in the province of Punjab was put down with severe violence by British troops. The local British commander in charge of the soldiers ordered his men to fire into the crowd – killing 379 Indian men, women and children.

The Amritsar incident was a turning point for the Indian National Congress and its leader, Mohandas Ghandi. He wrote, 'when a government takes up arms against its unarmed subjects, then it has lost the right to govern'. The Congress, more loudly than ever, demanded an independent India.

> **Source E** A photograph of Ghandi, taken in 1925. Every day he span cotton on a small spinning wheel to encourage people to lead simple lives. He wanted Indians to be proud of their country and realise that they didn't need British rule to survive.

Ghandi, a holy man and a very clever politician, told Indians to do all they could to make life difficult for the British, *without using violence*. Today, this is called **passive resistance**. Ghandi called it 'satyagraha', which means 'soul force pure and simple'. He encouraged strikes, demonstrations and **boycotts** (for example, asking Indians not to buy any goods made in Britain). His most famous protest occurred in 1930 when he began a campaign against the salt tax. At the time, Indians were not allowed to make their own salt – they had to buy it – and it was heavily taxed by the British Government. Ghandi led thousands of Indians to the coast where they began making salt from seawater. All over India, Indians copied Ghandi's example until, after putting 100 000 people in prison, the British gave in and got rid of the salt tax. By 1935, after many years of non-violent (and in some cases violent) protests, the Government of India Act gave Indians the right to control everything except the army. India, however, was still part of the British Empire and was still ruled by a viceroy. Many Indians, including Ghandi, continued to demand complete independence.

> **Source F** Who governs us? Part of a leaflet written by an anti-British group of Indians

'Can these thieves really be our rulers? These thieves ... import a huge number of goods made in their own country and sell them in our markets, stealing our wealth and taking life from our people. Can those who steal the harvest of our fields and doom us to hunger, fever and plague, really be our rulers? Can foreigners really be our rulers?'

WORK

1. a How did India contribute to the Great War?
   b What changes were made to the way the British governed India after the Great War?
   c Why were some Indians happy with these changes?
   d Why were others disappointed?
   e What happened in Amritsar in 1919?

2. Look at **Source E**.
   a Why did Mohandas Ghandi lead such a simple life?
   b Why do you think his protest against the salt tax annoyed the British so much?
   c Was Ghandi pleased with the Government of India Act? Explain your answer carefully.

3. Look at **Source F**. This leaflet was published by people who were *against* British rule in India.
   a Who are the 'thieves' mentioned in the leaflet?
   b Why do you think the writer hates the 'thieves' so much?

123

In 1939, when World War Two began, India was still part of the British Empire. Like in World War One, thousands of Indians joined up to fight as part of the British Empire force. In total, 2.5 million Indians fought in what was the largest volunteer army in history.

▼ **Source G** Indian soldiers with a captured German cannon in the Libyan desert in 1943

After the war, it was clear that Britain would have to give India its independence. Britain wasn't strong enough to hold on to a country so desperate to rule itself – and the people in Britain, tired of war, weren't keen to see their soldiers trying to control marches and demonstrations that so easily turned to violence!

But the whole matter of independence was complicated by the increasing violence between Hindus and Muslims. Relations had been bad for a long time, but after 1945, they started to break down completely. If India gained its independence, Muslims didn't want to be ruled by a mainly Hindu government (remember, there were a lot more Hindus in India than Muslims – see **Source B**). Instead, Muslims wanted a country of their own, made from areas where people were Muslims. They were to name this new country after these areas – P for Punjab, A for Afghanis, K for Kashmir, S for Sind and TAN for Baluchistan. The word PAKISTAN means 'land of the pure' in Urdu.

▼ **Source H** From a 1944 interview with Mohammed Ali Jinnah, the leader of an Indian political party called the Muslim League. He eventually became Pakistan's first leader.

'How can you even dream of Hindu–Muslim unity? Everything pulls us apart. We have no inter-marriages. We do not have the same calendar. The Muslims believe in a single God, the Hindus worship idols... The Hindus worship animals and consider cows sacred. We, the Muslims, think it is nonsense. We want to kill the cows and eat them. There are only two links between the Muslims and Hindus: British rule – and the common desire to get rid of it.'

As violence between Muslims and Hindus continued, the British hurriedly made plans to split India into two countries – India would be for Hindus and Pakistan would be for Muslims. The millions of Sikhs, who felt they didn't belong in either, would have to choose one or the other.

On 15 August 1947, Britain stopped ruling India. The whole sub-continent was divided into Hindu India and Muslim Pakistan (itself divided into two parts – see **Source I**). Immediately there were problems. As it was impossible to make sure that the boundaries were drawn so that all Muslims were in Pakistan and all Hindus were in India, millions now found themselves in the wrong country. As they fled across the boundaries to be in the country of their religion, whole trainloads were massacred by the 'other' side. Nobody knows exactly how many were killed, but some have estimated as many as one million! Then, at the height of this violence and bloodshed, Ghandi himself, the man who had believed in non-violence, was assassinated by an **extremist** Hindu.

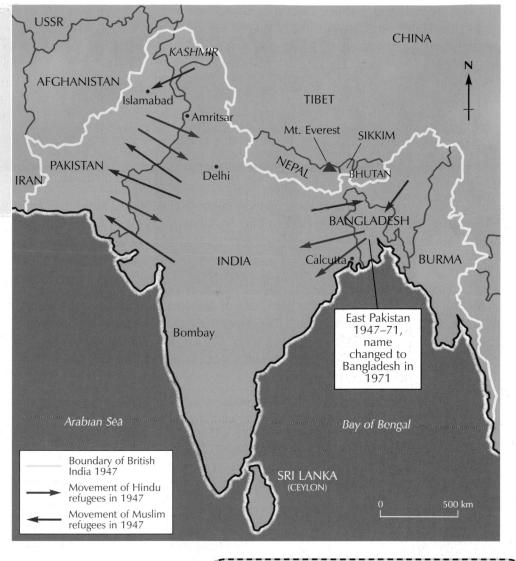

▶ **Source I** How India was divided. Areas where more than half the people were Muslim became Pakistan whilst areas where over half the population were Hindu became India. This left millions in the 'wrong' country. It has been estimated that over 14 million fled to the 'other side' in 1947. Thousands from both religions were slaughtered on the way.

The troubled start for the new, independent nations of India and Pakistan continued. Major differences continue to this day.

The cost of World War Two in terms of money, lives and buildings meant that the British Government had to concentrate on rebuilding Britain itself. As the Empire took a back seat, many colonies, like India, under British rule demanded their independence. Today, the British Empire consists of a few loyal islands.

Map labels:
USSR, CHINA, KASHMIR, AFGHANISTAN, Islamabad, Amritsar, TIBET, Mt. Everest, SIKKIM, NEPAL, BHUTAN, PAKISTAN, IRAN, Delhi, BANGLADESH, INDIA, Calcutta, BURMA, Bombay, East Pakistan 1947–71, name changed to Bangladesh in 1971, Arabian Sea, Bay of Bengal, SRI LANKA (CEYLON)

Boundary of British India 1947
Movement of Hindu refugees in 1947
Movement of Muslim refugees in 1947
0   500 km

WISE UP WORDS

passive resistance   boycott   extremist

HUNGRY FOR MORE?

Find out what's left of the British Empire.

Which countries or colonies are still part of the British Empire?

Make a timeline showing when different nations gained their independence from Britain.

What is the British Commonwealth?

WORK

1 a Why was India split into two countries in 1947?
   b How did Pakistan get its name?
   c Why did there continue to be violence between Hindus and Muslims even after India and Pakistan became separate countries?
   d What do you think Sikh people disliked about the new countries and borders?

2 Look at **Source H**.
   a Who was Mohammed Ali Jinnah?
   b In your own words, explain why Jinnah thought that unity between Hindus and Muslims was impossible.

3 Many historians say that Britain lost its Empire because of its involvement in two world wars. Do you agree with this view? Use the information on these six pages to support your answer.

Martin Luther King Junior and his followers continued to organise marches, boycotts and demonstrations wherever local laws discriminated against blacks. One year, Martin Luther King Junior himself travelled 780 000 miles and made 208 speeches campaigning for equal rights. These people were called 'civil rights protesters' because they called for the same *rights* as ordinary white *civilians*. In 1961, they organised a famous 'freedom ride' from Washington to New Orleans. Using Rosa Park's example, protesters travelled on a series of buses and on each one, they sat in the 'whites only' section.

Sometimes they organised 'sit-ins' where they refused to leave a 'whites only' restaurant until they were seated. First started by black students at a Woolworth's food counter in 1960, 70 000 other people had tried similar protests all over America by 1961.

Throughout the whole civil rights struggle, King insisted on peaceful protest and urged his followers not to fight back when attacked: 'we must meet violence with non-violence', he said.

TWENTY CENTS

FEBRUARY 18, 1957

TIME
THE WEEKLY NEWSMAGAZINE

Montgomery, Alabama's
REV. MARTIN LUTHER KING

VOL. LXIX NO. 7

$6.00 A YEAR

◀ **Source C** One of the February 1968 covers of *Time*, America's largest-selling weekly magazine. It shows a picture of Martin Luther King Junior and, if you look carefully, you can see a photograph of the Montgomery Bus Boycott in the bottom left-hand corner.

Source D The words of Martin Luther King, 28 August 1963

'I have a dream that one day this nation will rise up and live out the true meaning of its creed [beliefs] … that all men are created equal. I have a dream that one day my four little children will live in a nation where they will not be judged by the colour of their skin but by the content of their character. I have a dream. When we allow freedom to ring from every town and every hamlet [village], from every state and every city, we will be able to speed up the day when all God's children, black and white, Jews and Gentiles [non-Jewish people], Protestants and Catholics, will be able to join hands and sing in the words of that old Negro spiritual, "Free at last! Free at last! Great God Almighty, we are free at last!"'

FACT: ▶ Black is beautiful

▶ Not all black people supported Martin Luther King Junior – they disagreed with his non-violent approach. The most famous of these was Malcolm X, who adopted the Muslim religion because he felt it was one that non-white people could feel was their own. One of his most famous followers was the world's heavyweight boxing champion Cassius Clay, who changed his name to Mohamed Ali, a Muslim name. He felt that Clay was a slave name given to his ancestors by slave owners who brought them from Africa. Ali was well known for saying, amongst other things, 'I'm black and I'm proud'.

On 28 August 1963, King spoke to 250 000 people at a massive rally in Washington and gave one of the most famous speeches in history (see **Source D**). As a result of the pressure from King and other civil rights **activists**, the American government finally began to change the law. The Civil Rights Act of 1964 made racial discrimination illegal. A year later, the Voting Act gave equal rights to all black and white people throughout America.

But despite the great strides made in the area of civil rights, laws cannot change people's minds. In many ways, America remains a divided society today. King himself was shot dead by a white racist in 1968 and King's dream of a peaceful, multiracial society is far from reality. Individual black Americans – lawyers, sports stars, musicians, doctors – have enjoyed glittering careers but at the start of the twenty-first century, the average black family earned just about half the wage of an average white family. But King's dreams still live on.

WISE UP WORDS

segregation   activists   civil rights

WORK

1 a Why were Martin Luther King Junior and his followers called 'civil rights protesters'?
   b What other methods, apart from the Montgomery Bus Boycott, did civil rights protesters use in the campaign to gain equal rights?
   c What was Martin Luther King Junior's attitude to violent protest?
   d Suggest reasons why Martin Luther King Junior did not want to use violence.

2 a Write a sentence or two about: i) The Civil Rights Act, 1964 ii) The Voting Act, 1965.
   b In what way is the USA *still* divided?
   c If America is still divided, does that mean that Martin Luther King Junior was a failure? Explain your answer carefully.

3 Look at **Source D**.
   a In your own words, try to sum up Martin Luther King Junior's 'dream'. What was his dream for the future?
   b What is your dream for the future? Write your own speech, using Martin Luther King Junior's as your inspiration.

What is terrorism?

▸ What are some of the causes of **terrorism**?
▸ How do **terrorists** attack and what can be done to prevent them?

On the morning of 11 September 2001, 19 terrorists hijacked four American passenger planes. After taking control, the hijackers flew two of the aircraft straight into two of the tallest buildings in New York City – the twin towers of the World Trade Center, two skyscrapers containing thousands of office workers.

A third plane with 64 passengers on board was flown into the Pentagon building in Washington, the headquarters of the US army, navy and air force. Half an hour later, the fourth plane crashed in a field near Pennsylvania, not far from Washington. Many experts believe it was heading for the White House, the home of the US President. The fourth flight never made it because some of the 38 passengers fought with the hijackers to stop them reaching their target.

The US President, George W Bush, was visiting a school when he heard of the attacks. In a statement a few hours later, he said that 'a national tragedy has occurred today. Two aeroplanes have crashed into the World Trade Center in a terrorist attack on our country'.

But what exactly is terrorism? How, when and where have terrorists attacked in the past? And how, if at all, can terrorists be stopped?

◂ **Source A** The front page of *The Sun* newspaper from 12 September 2001. The photo shows the second plane hitting the World Trade Center.

▾ **Source B** Part of President Bush's television statement, read out on the evening of 11 September 2001. What do you think the final line of his speech means?

'Today our fellow citizens, our way of life, our very freedom came under attack in a series of deliberate and deadly terrorist attacks. These acts of mass murder were intended to frighten our nation into chaos and defeat. Thousands of lives were suddenly ended by evil, despicable acts of terror ... our military is powerful and it is prepared. The search is under way for those who committed this evil act. We will make no distinction between the terrorists who committed these acts and those who harboured them.'

Terrorism is the use of violence and intimidation for political reasons. Terrorists want to change the way governments and politicians behave by using threats, fear and bloodshed – in other words, terror. Terrorists don't usually represent a large proportion of the population so never get enough support for their ideas by normal peaceful methods. Instead, they try to frighten people into behaving the way they want.

▶ **Source C** A timeline of events on 11 September 2001. In total, over 3 000 people died in the attacks.

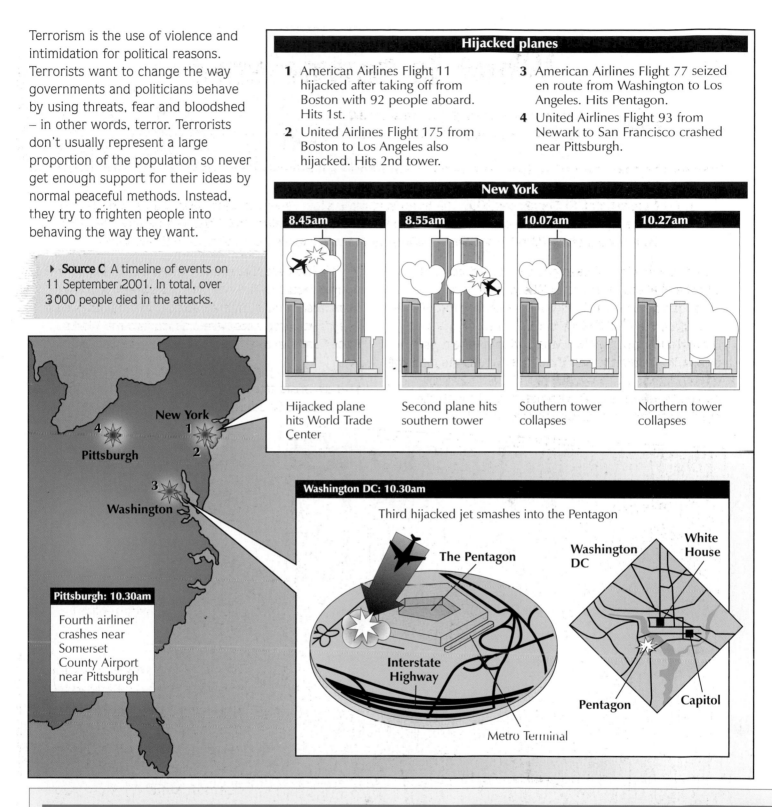

Hijacked planes

1 American Airlines Flight 11 hijacked after taking off from Boston with 92 people aboard. Hits 1st.

2 United Airlines Flight 175 from Boston to Los Angeles also hijacked. Hits 2nd tower.

3 American Airlines Flight 77 seized en route from Washington to Los Angeles. Hits Pentagon.

4 United Airlines Flight 93 from Newark to San Francisco crashed near Pittsburgh.

New York

8.45am — Hijacked plane hits World Trade Center

8.55am — Second plane hits southern tower

10.07am — Southern tower collapses

10.27am — Northern tower collapses

Pittsburgh: 10.30am
Fourth airliner crashes near Somerset County Airport near Pittsburgh

Washington DC: 10.30am
Third hijacked jet smashes into the Pentagon

The Pentagon
Interstate Highway
Metro Terminal

Washington DC — White House — Pentagon — Capitol

WORK

1 Why do you think the terrorists chose as their target: i) The World Trade Center ii) The Pentagon iii) The White House?

2 a In your own words, explain what is meant by the word 'terrorism'.

   b What is a 'terrorist'?

3 a Make your own timeline of events for the terrorist attacks on America on 11 September 2001.

   b Why do you think many people criticised the American government's security services after the attacks?

The attacks on the World Trade Center and the Pentagon in September 2001 were two more in a series of attacks by one of the world's most famous terrorist groups, al-Qaeda. This mysterious group's members, led by a millionaire Saudi Arabian named Osama Bin Laden, are all followers of Islam but have very strict, extremist beliefs that are different from Muslims living in Britain. They believe they are fighting a holy war, or **jihad**, against enemies of their religion.

America, in particular, is seen as one of al-Qaeda's greatest enemies. They dislike America because they believe Americans interfere too much in the Middle East, the area around the eastern Mediterranean Sea including Kuwait, Iran, Iraq, Israel, Syria, Jordan, Saudi Arabia and so on. The Middle East is the source of 60% of the world's oil. In today's modern world, oil is essential, especially for nearly all forms of transport. American cars, trucks, trains as well as homes and factories all need this oil – as a result, America is very interested in what happens in this area.

For many years, America has kept battleships and built airbases in some Middle Eastern countries, most notably Saudi Arabia. Not just al-Qaeda but many other countries find the American presence in the Middle East threatening. Al-Qaeda also targeted America because they believe they helped enemies of Islam, like Israeli Jews, during wars against Muslim nations in the Middle East. Al-Qaeda want American influence out of the Middle East and are prepared to use terrorism to either frighten America into leaving or anger them so much that the US starts a holy war against all Muslim states. This, al-Qaeda hope, will end with final victory for Islam.

FACT: ▶ Osama Bin Laden

▶ Born in 1957, 17th son of a very rich family

Grew up in Jeddah, Saudi Arabia

Has more than 50 brothers and sisters

Al-Qaeda (which means 'the base') set up in 1989 in Afghanistan to fight people who were seen as enemies of Islam

Has used his money to run his global terror network

▲ **Source D** Until the 11 September attacks, al-Qaeda had mainly used car bombs. Other attacks include a bombing of the World Trade Center in 1993, killing six, and bombings of the US embassies in Kenya and in Tanzania, killing 234 people. This photograph shows rescue workers helping victims after the 1998 bombing in Kenya.

Terrorism has been used for many, many years to try to achieve a wide variety of different aims and objectives. Sometimes the terrorists have political causes – they say they represent a group that want their own country, for example – whilst other terrorists have religious causes like al-Qaeda. More often than not though, terrorism is used for a mixture of religious and political reasons.

WORK

1 Write a sentence or two to explain the following terms:
   extremist • jihad • al-Qaeda

2 a What do you think is meant by the term 'anti-American'?

   b Why is al-Qaeda so anti-American?

133

Glossary

Activist A person who works energetically to achieve political or social goals.

Alliance An agreement between countries.

Allies Countries on the same side.

Anti-Semitism The hatred and persecution of Jews.

Appeasement The policy of giving someone what they want in the hope that their demands will stop.

Area bombing Whole towns or cities bombed in an attempt to make sure that everything is destroyed.

Artillery Large guns or cannon.

Aryan A person of German or Scandinavian origin, usually fair-haired and blue eyed. The Nazis believed that Aryans were superior to all other races.

Assassination The murder of an important or well known person.

Assembly line A system for making goods in a factory; the product is put together stage by stage.

Asylum Refuge or a safe place.

Attrition Gradually wearing down.

Bayonet A long knife that fits on the end of a rifle.

Big Three (The) The leaders of Britain, France and the USA – the most powerful winning countries at the end of the war.

Boycott A boycott happens when people refuse to buy goods from a particular shop or business.

Brittle Hard but easily broken.

Ceasefire An agreement that stops two sides fighting each other.

Censor To cut out or erase.

Censorship The cutting out or banning of books, plays, films, newspapers or anything that a government does not wish to have expressed.

Chancellor German or Austrian term for Prime Minister.

Charter i) a document that demands or grants certain rights ii) the basic rules and regulations of an organisation.

Chlorine gas A strong-smelling, greenish-yellow gas that affects a soldier's breathing, causing him to choke – can kill.

Civilians People not in the army, navy or air force.

Civil rights Equal rights, for example, the right to vote, which are available to all.

Cold War (The) A state of tension – but not actual war – between the USSR and the USA and her allies between 1945 and 1991.

Communism A political system where all property is owned by the government; people are equal and they are paid by the government according to their needs.

Communist A person who lives in a country where the government follows the political system known as Communism.

Concentration camp A harsh camp for civilian prisoners.

Conscientious objector Someone who is against war and refuses to help the armed forces.

Conscription The policy of forcing men to join the army, navy or air force.

Court martial A military court for trying soldiers.

Cowardice Lack of courage.

Democracy A way of running a country in which the government is chosen by the people.

Desertion Abandoning a place without intending to return. This was a serious offence for a soldier.

Dictator A ruler with total control over how a country is governed.

Dictatorship A country ruled by a dictator.

Duckboard A cover for the muddy trench floor.

Eastern Front An area where Russians fought against Germans and Austrians.

Eugenics The study of methods of improving the human race.

Evacuation Being taken from a high-risk area to somewhere safer.

Extremist A person who holds excessive religious or political views.

Fascism A system of government that is against democracy and personal freedom and supports a strong, aggressive army, navy and air force.

Fascist Someone who is against democracy and believes in rule by one powerful leader, supported by a strong army, navy and air force.

Firestep The raised platform that a soldier stands on to fire at the enemy.

Firestorm A 'super-heated' fire where winds reach speeds of 120 miles per hour.

Flame thrower A specially adapted gun that can shoot a flame over 15 metres.

Führer German word for 'leader', used by Hitler as leader of Nazi Germany.

Genocide Murder of a race of people.

Gestapo German secret police.

Ghetto A small, sealed-off section of a town or city in which Jews were forced to live.

Great Depression (The)   The period in the 1930s when there was high unemployment because many companies were out of business.

Hand grenades   A bomb thrown by hand.

Hereditary   Passed on genetically from one generation to another.

Holocaust   Usually used to describe the murder of millions of Jews by the Nazis during World War Two.

Hull   The bottom of a ship.

Hunger strike   Not eating as a way of protesting.

Incendiary   Bombs specially designed to start fires.

Indoctrinated   Another word for 'brainwashing' – to teach someone to accept a belief without question.

Infamous   Well known for something bad.

Jihad   Islamic holy war against unbelievers.

Kamikaze   Japanese suicide pilots.

League of Nations   An international peace-keeping organisation set up at the end of the Great War.

Lice   Parasites that live on the skin and feed off blood.

Maiden voyage   A ship's first trip out to sea.

Martyr   A person who would die for his or her beliefs.

Mass-production   The production of goods in huge numbers, usually making them cheaper.

Mass rallies   Huge meetings.

Mein Kampf   A book written by Hitler containing his views.

Militant   Aggressive or violent in support of a cause.

Munitions   Materials used in war, such as guns, bullets and shells.

Mustard gas   A poisonous gas causing blistering burns and blindness.

National Insurance   A system organised by the Government to insure people against sickness, injury and so on.

No man's land   The wasteland between two opposing sides during a war that neither side controls.

Parapet   The top of a trench.

Pardon   Official release from punishment for a crime.

Passive resistance   To protect against government, law and so on by non-violent acts.

Patriotism   Supporting your country, especially against its enemies.

Periscope   A mirrored instrument used to give a view of something at a different level.

Persecution   Treating someone cruelly because of race, religion and so on.

Precision bombing   Careful, precise bombing of military targets, such as munitions factories or navy dockyards.

Propaganda   Persuading people to believe something, even by telling them lies.

Rearmament   Building up a country's weapons and armed forces again.

Recruitment   The attempt to persuade men to join the army, navy or air force.

Retreat   Move back from a position.

Segregation   The policy of keeping black and white Americans apart by giving them separate facilities, such as schools and hospitals.

Shares   Small parts of a company, bought by a shareholder who hopes to make a profit if the company does well.

Shell   A bomb fired from a large gun.

Shell-shock   A nervous disorder caused by long exposure to battle conditions.

Slump   A bad or sudden drop in trade.

Snipers   Soldiers who shoot from a hiding place.

Social security   Help for people with little or no income.

Stalemate   A deadlock in a battle situation where neither side makes any progress.

Steerage   Third-class passengers on a ship.

Sterilised   A sterilised person has undergone an operation to make them unable to produce children.

Storm troopers   The nickname for the SA, Hitler's private army of brown-shirted thugs.

Suffrage   The right to vote.

Suffragette   A campaigner for the right of women to vote; often prepared to use violence to get their message across.

Superpowers   A term used to describe the world's two most powerful nations – the USA and the USSR – during the Cold War.

Swastika   The crooked cross symbol adopted by the Nazi Party as their emblem.

Terrorism   The use of violence and intimidation to achieve political aims.

Terrorist   A person who uses violence and intimidation to achieve political aims.

Treaty   An agreement between countries.

Trench foot   A foot disease caused by standing in the cold and wet.

Triple Alliance   The leaders from Germany, Austria-Hungary and Italy, among others.

Triple Entente   The leaders from Britain, France and Russia, among others.

Vengeance   Revenge.

Welfare state   A system by which the Government looks after the well-being of the nation, particularly those who cannot help themselves, such as the old, children, the sick, unemployed and so on.

Western Front   In Belgium and France, where French, British and Belgium soldiers protected the channel coast from the Germans.

Index

al-Qaeda 132, 133, 134, 135
anti-Semitism 100
appeasement 85
area bombing 94, 96
Armstrong, Neil 116
Aryans 68, 79
attrition 40
Auschwitz 98, 99, 100, 101, 102, 103

Battle of Britain 87, 88, 89
Battle of the Somme, 1916 21, 40, 41
Beveridge, Sir William 114, 115
Bin Laden, Osama 132
birth control 136, 139
Blitz, the 89, 93
bombs/bombing 23, 87, 90, 93, 94, 95, 96, 97, 104, 105, 106, 107, 113, 127, 134
boycotts 123, 126, 127, 128
British Empire 4, 34, 120, 121, 122, 123, 124, 125, 138

Capitalism 110, 111, 113
cars 6, 19, 23, 77, 132, 137
ceasefire 48
censorship 77
Chamberlain, Neville 84, 85
children/young people 8, 9, 17, 74, 75, 76, 90, 91, 92, 93, 97, 99, 114, 115, 136, 137
Churchill, Winston 8, 83, 85, 86, 89, 96, 110, 114, 115
civil rights activists/protesters 128, 129
class differences 5, 10, 11, 12, 14, 15, 16, 18, 19
Cold War 111, 112, 113
Communism 60, 61, 62, 71, 77, 110, 111, 112, 113
concentration/extermination camps 72, 98, 99, 100, 101, 102, 103
conscientious objectors 27
conscription 27
Conservative Party 9, 114
cowardice 26, 44, 45, 46, 47
Cuban missile crisis 112, 113
Curie, Marie 7

democracy 58, 59
desertion 44, 47
dictatorship 58, 59, 60, 61, 62
'dole', the 9, 114
Dresden 94, 95, 96, 97

Eastern Front 29
education 74, 75, 137, 138
Edward VII 4, 121
evacuation 90, 91, 92, 93

Fascism 60, 62
Ferdinand, Franz (Archduke) 22, 23, 24
'final solution', the 98, 102, 103

gas 36, 37, 66, 100
genocide 103
George V 49
Gestapo 72
Ghandi, Mohandas 123, 124
ghettoes 98
Government of Britain 5, 8, 26, 27, 49, 52, 90, 93, 94, 114, 115, 122, 123, 125, 135, 137
government types 58, 59, 60, 62, 111
Great Depression, the 70, 71

Haig, Sir Douglas 40, 42, 46, 47
Harris, Sir Arthur 94, 95, 96, 97
hijacking 130, 134
Hitler, Adolf 57, 62, 64, 65, 66, 67, 68, 69, 70, 71, 72, 73, 74, 75, 76, 77, 78, 79, 82, 83, 84, 85, 86, 87, 89, 98, 105
Holocaust, the 102
hunger strike 52

illness 7, 8, 33, 44, 45, 108, 109, 136, 137
India 120, 121, 122, 123, 136
Irish Republic Army (IRA) 135
'Iron Curtain' 110

Japan 104, 105, 106, 107
Jews 64, 66, 68, 72, 73, 74, 77, 78, 98, 99, 100, 101, 102, 103, 132
jihad 132

Labour Party 9, 114, 115
League of Nations 56, 57
Liberal Party 8, 9
lice 33, 35, 65, 92
Lloyd George, David 8, 56
Luftwaffe 87, 89
Luther King, Martin (Junior) 126, 127, 128, 129

Marx, Karl 60
moon landings 116, 117, 118, 119
Mussolini, Benito 62, 63

National Health Service (NHS) 115, 137
Nazis 67, 68, 69, 70, 71, 72, 73, 74, 75, 76, 77, 78, 79, 98, 99, 101, 102, 103, 110
newspapers 6, 16, 26, 48, 55, 59, 61, 69, 103, 116, 130
no man's land 29, 30, 38
nuclear weapons 104, 105, 106, 107, 111, 112, 113

Olympic Games 7, 78, 79
'Operation Sealion' 86, 87, 88, 89

Pakistan 124, 125
Parks, Rosa 126, 127
Parliament 52, 53, 56, 58, 83
passive resistance 123
patriotism 26
Pearl Harbor 104, 105, 106
pensions 9, 114, 115, 137
precision bombing 94
Princip, Gavrilo 22, 23, 24
propaganda 26, 27, 77

racism 62, 72, 126, 128, 129
RAF (Royal Air Force) 87, 88, 89, 94, 97
recruitment 26
religion 58, 59, 61, 76, 120, 121, 124, 125, 129, 132, 133, 135, 136
Remembrance Day 49

segregation 126
shells 37, 40, 41, 44
shell-shock 37, 44, 47
stalemate 29
Stalin, Joseph 61, 85, 111
storm troopers 68
suffragettes 52, 53
swastika 69, 78

tanks 38, 40, 43, 68, 71, 82, 110
taxes 115, 122, 123
terrorism 130, 131, 132, 133, 134, 135
terrorist weapons 134, 135
Titanic 10, 11, 12, 13, 14, 15, 16, 17, 18, 19
Treaty of Versailles 56, 57, 68, 82
trench foot 33
trench warfare 28–42, 49, 66, 122

United Nations (UN) 108, 109

Victoria, Queen 4, 120
vote 52, 53

war, effects of 48, 49, 53, 56, 57, 60, 68, 82, 93, 108, 109, 110, 124, 125, 138
war planes 87, 88, 89, 94, 95, 96, 97, 104, 105
welfare state 114, 115
Western Front 29, 42
women 5, 7, 17, 52, 53, 76, 97, 99, 137, 138, 139
World War One (the Great War) 20–49, 53, 56, 57, 59, 60, 66, 82, 122
World War Two 58, 59, 64, 82, 83, 85, 86–108, 110, 114, 120, 124
Wright brothers 6